KW-360-151

The Social Market Foundation

The Foundation's main activity is to commission and publish original papers by independent academic and other experts on key topics in the economic and social fields, with a view to stimulating public discussion on the performance of markets and the social framework within which they operate. The Foundation is a registered charity and a company limited by guarantee. It is independent of any political party or group and is financed by the sale of publications and by voluntary donations from individuals, organisations and companies. The views expressed in publications are those of the authors and do not represent a corporate opinion of the Foundation.

Chairman
David Lipsey (Lord Lipsey of Tooting Bec)

Members of the Board
Viscount Chandos
Gavyn Davies
David Edmonds
Martin Ivens
Brian Pomeroy
Shriti Vadera

Director
Ann Rossiter

First published by
The Social Market Foundation,
April 2007

The Social Market Foundation
11 Tufton Street
London SW1P 3QB

Designed by www.jadedesign.net

Contents

About the authors

Ann Rossiter, Social Market Foundation
Ann Rossiter joined the SMF in July 2003 as Director of
Research and in February 2004 also took on the role of Acting
Director before being appointed as Director in July 2005.
Before joining the SMF, her career included a number of
advisory roles in politics and policymaking. She spent four years
at the BBC in the Political Research Unit and in political pro-
gramming, followed by four years working in parliament for
Rt Hon John Denham MP and Glenda Jackson MP, on
pensions and transport policy. She is a specialist in pensions
policy and welfare reform. Other policy interests include
employment and the operation of markets. Prior to joining
the SMF, Ann worked for four years as a Director of Fishburn
Hedges, the corporate communications consultancy, and for
Lexington Communications.

Jim Murphy MP, Department for Work and Pensions
Jim Murphy is the Minister of State for Employment and
Welfare Reform at the Department for Work and Pensions,
a position he has held since May 2006. He was previously
appointed Parliamentary Secretary at the Cabinet Office follow-
ing the General Election in May 2005. He was Parliamentary
Private Secretary to the Secretary of State for Scotland from
March 2001 until June 2002, when he was appointed to the
government as a whip. Jim Murphy entered Parliament in
May 1997 as MP for East Renfrewshire. He has enjoyed the
biggest electoral swing from Conservative to Labour of any
MP in Britain over the past decade.

Dr Jo Blanden, University of Surrey and Centre for Economic Performance, LSE

Jo Blanden is a lecturer in economics at the University of Surrey, a position she was appointed to in 2005. Previous to this, she spent five years as a researcher at the Centre for Economic Performance (CEP) at the London School of Economics, where she remains a research associate. Her research interests lie in family and labour economics. The majority of her work to date has investigated the impact of family background on future life chances. She has also written on UK industrial relations.

Lisa Harker, Department for Work and Pensions

Lisa Harker is an independent policy adviser specialising in issues related to families, poverty and social exclusion. In June 2006 she was appointed as an adviser on child poverty to the Department for Work and Pensions and her report 'Delivering on Child Poverty: What would it take?' was published in November 2006. She was previously Deputy Director of the Institute of Public Policy Research (2000-03), Chair of the Daycare Trust (2001-06) and is a director of Aspire Oxfordshire, a social enterprise that provides employment opportunities for homeless people.

Professor Paul Gregg and Lindsey Macmillan, University of Bristol

Paul Gregg is a professor in the Department of Economics, University of Bristol. He is also a member of the London Child Poverty Commission and a programme director at the Centre for Market and Public Organisation. Lindsey Macmillan is a research assistant at the Centre for Market and Public Organisation, University of Bristol.

Dr Roy Sainsbury, University of York

Roy Sainsbury is an assistant director of the Social Policy Research Unit at the University of York. His research projects have included work on sickness and disability, employment policy and social security benefits. Current work includes the evaluation of the Pathways to Work pilots.

Trevor Phillips, Commission for Equality and Human Rights
Trevor Phillips is Chair of the new Commission for Equality
and Human Rights, which will take over the work of Britain's
three existing equality commissions as well as new responsibilities for equality and human rights in October 2007. Previously
Trevor was Chair of the Commission for Racial Equality.
Between 2000 and 2003, he was Chair of the Greater London
Authority. Born in London in 1953, Trevor attended secondary school in Georgetown, Guyana, and then studied chemistry
at Imperial College London. Between 1978 and 1980, he was
president of the National Union of Students. He then went
into broadcasting, becoming Head of Current Affairs at LWT
in 1992. In addition to many newspaper articles and comment
pieces, Trevor has co-written books on ethnicity and on the history of slavery.

Sir Jonathan Sacks, Chief Rabbi
Sir Jonathan Sacks has been the Chief Rabbi of the United
Hebrew congregations of the Commonwealth since 1991. He
has earned international acclaim, both as a scholar and spiritual
leader. At his installation as Chief Rabbi in 1991, Dr Sacks set
out his vision of a reinvigorated Anglo-Jewry and launched it
with a Decade of Jewish Renewal, followed by a series of innovative communal projects. In September 2001 he began his
second decade of office with a call to Jewish responsibility and a
renewed commitment to the ethical dimensions of Judaism. He
was awarded a knighthood in the Queen's birthday honours list
in June 2005. Rabbi Sacks is the author of many books and has
made numerous appearances on national radio, television and
press interviews.

Camila Batmanghelidjh, Kids Company
Camila Batmanghelidjh is founder and Director of Kids
Company, a charity that delivers practical and therapeutic interventions to vulnerable inner-city children through 32 inner
London schools, a children's centre and an urban academy. She
also set up The Place2Be, which offers emotional support and
therapy in primary schools. Camila was born in Tehran and
educated as a psychotherapist in the UK. She has more than six-

teen years of psychoanalytic experience and has written widely in this area.

Sir Dexter Hutt, Ninestiles Federation

Dexter Hutt attended schools in Guyana and England before graduating from Birmingham University. After leaving university he taught in Handsworth and Coventry before taking up the headship of Ninestiles School in Birmingham in 1988. Ninestiles progressed from being a failing school to a top performer, and Dexter received a knighthood for his services to education. He is heavily involved in school improvement, both regionally and with the DfES. He is now Executive Headteacher of the Ninestiles Federation of Schools and Chief Executive of its training and consultancy company, Ninestiles Plus, which has supported school improvement in schools both nationally and internationally in Indiana and Cape Town. Dexter Hutt is also a commissioner for the Commission for Racial Equality.

Dr Simon Griffiths, Social Market Foundation

Simon Griffiths joined the SMF as Senior Research Fellow in January 2007 after completing a doctorate at the London School of Economics on the adoption of pro-market arguments amongst the British left during the 1980s and 1990s, issues on which he has published in major journals and in the media. He previously worked as a parliamentary researcher, taught politics at LSE, and carried out academic research in various capacities for the sociologist, Anthony Giddens. He focuses on public service reform for the SMF and is editor of the current collection.

Preface

Historically, one of the defining political differences between those on the right and those on the left has been attitudes towards aspiration. The traditional response from the right has been to promote and encourage personal ambition but to regard this solely as a factor of personal effort. This "pulling yourself up by your bootstraps" approach to the politics of aspiration neglects the important and sometimes overwhelming barriers that stand in the way of both individual aspiration and its achievements. On the other hand, the traditional, class-based, political analysis of the old left has tended to prove unattractive to voters from all classes because it seemed to recognise those social and economic barriers without acknowledging the validity of the impulse to improve the lot of yourself and your family.

The complex interaction of forces and circumstances that conspires to keep those who are born in poverty in the same situation for the duration of their lives, and which make social exclusion a transgenerational phenomenon, is the subject of this collection. It presumes that fighting social exclusion is both an ethical and an economic imperative: we have an obligation to address those conditions that prevent individuals from fulfilling their capabilities irrespective of their start in life, and which prevent them imagining and achieving a different kind of future. Fairness in life chances is taken to be the primary objective.

In coming to power, the New Labour government recognised that it needed to take seriously the aspirations of citizens from all backgrounds but also that, for many people, the barriers to personal and family achievement were overwhelming. Considerable effort has been expended in identifying and dismantling those barriers through a range of mechanisms,

1 J Gershuny, *Beating the Odds (1): Intergenerational social mobility from a human capital perspective* and *Beating the Odds (2): A new index of intergenerational social mobility* (Institute for Social and Economic Research; Strategy Unit Report, 2002).

2 J Hills, and K Stewart (eds.), *A More Equal Society? New Labour, poverty, inequality and exclusion* (The Policy Press, 2005).

including the national minimum wage, Sure Start, the Child Trust Fund, education reforms, active labour market policies, and the system of tax credits.

The impact that the New Labour government will have had on social mobility will not be fully understood for at least a generation. However there are indications that social mobility is slowing or even going in the wrong direction.[1] Certainly the gap between rich and poor is worsening, albeit not to the degree that would have been the case without the initiatives the government has undertaken.[2] This suggests that further effort to identify and dismantle the barriers that prevent all citizens realising their potential should remain an important objective for Labour as it nears the mid-point of its third term in office.

The purpose of the collection of essays commissioned here is to deepen political understanding of the barriers to further social mobility and to the realising of personal aspiration, particularly among the most disadvantaged sections of society, and to identify further steps that the government can take to overcome these barriers through clear, incisive analysis from leading experts in the field.

Ann Rossiter
Director
Social Market Foundation

1. Progressive self-interest – the politics of poverty and aspiration

Jim Murphy MP

Introduction

The politics of aspiration has always been the driving force behind political change. Across history it has sparked revolutions, driven social progress, created trade unions and political parties, and changed the destiny of continents.

Today in the UK the party that best responds to the changing nature of public aspiration will dominate the next decade. In truth the real prize will not go to those who follow aspiration but to those who anticipate and shape it.

Labour's history is a binary one. Labour is either the party of personal and collective aspiration or a party of opposition. As New Labour enters its second decade in power, we should embrace aspiration as a driver of further reform of public services. We should also use it to reframe the debate and public policy on eradicating poverty.

Historically, empowerment and aspiration have been integral to Labour governments' approach to public service reform – but for occasional political and intellectual spasms when we seemed unwilling to compromise with the electorate.

Both Tony Blair and Gordon Brown ensured that aspiration is part of the essential architecture of New Labour. It is no coincidence that our three election victories have been concurrent with the largest uninterrupted period that Labour has ever remained consistently connected to the nation's aspirations.

3 M Foot cited in N Timmins, *The Five Giants: A biography of the welfare state* (HarperCollins), p. 102.

4 Department of Education and Science, *The Organisation of Secondary Education, Circular 10/65*, ['The Crosland Circular'], (DES, 12 July 1965).

5 The Labour Party, *Time for Decision* (Election manifesto, 1966), Part 4, Section 4.

The Labour Party was born of the aspiration of an age. Almost half a century later when Bevan published the NHS Bill, he deliberately placed power in the hands of the patient rather than GPs when he prevented the buying and selling of GPs' patient rolls. As Michael Foot said: 'Bevan desperately wanted the patient to have choice of GP practice. He saw it as the best safeguard against poor service from the GP.'[3]

In 1965, Tony Crosland, Secretary of State for Education and Science at the time, published the *Organisation of Secondary Education* on the introduction of comprehensive education and the abolition of the 11-plus. In the text, Crosland pronounced that 'parents must have the final decision' over choice of secondary school. As a precursor to New Labour's choice advisers in schools and hospitals some four decades later, the Crosland circular added: 'but parents from less educated homes in particular should have a full explanation of the opportunities open to their children.'[4]

Innovation in public services has also traditionally been an essential component of Labour's approach to overcoming material and generational poverty. In 1966, with the creation of Jennie Lee's inspirational effort, the Open University, and with the wider expansion of the universities, Labour's manifesto proclaimed 'genuine equality of opportunity for millions of people for the first time.'[5] The introduction of family allowances by the Attlee government and child benefit by Wilson's government were also innovative, as was the way in which they were paid. Payments directly to the purse helped empower many working class mums.

No retreat from reform
The lessons of Labour history are also stark. If we stand still we will stagnate; momentum will be lost, possibly never to be recaptured. When the left has neglected challenges, the right has seen opportunity. When Gaitskill and others urged the party to make a property-owning democracy the social democratic objective, they were pilloried. Labour politicians first discussed building council houses for sale, but allowed a vacuum to be filled by a different solution to that challenge. We anticipated aspiration, but we failed to act. So again today it is Labour's role not only to match aspiration but also to anticipate it. And

in a world where so much is becoming global, local, personal solutions will be demanded of the public services in the future. Today, this happens in some areas, in some circumstances, but not universally.

In more recent times, we have made much greater use of competition from the private and voluntary sectors to drive up standards in all our public services. We have recognised the complex nature of disadvantage, and its corollary, that the monolithic structure of top-down services delivered from the centre will not effectively deal with the diversity of individual circumstances. And we've promoted local initiatives to focus on local solutions.

When people talk of change and reform in the context of government and the public sector, some talk of 'reform fatigue'. They talk about reform as if there is an end point. There never will be. We need to continue to adapt services to new challenges. When the modern welfare state was created, the service side of the private sector in Britain was embryonic. People's attitudes to services were shaped by their public sector experience. This has not been the case for some time now. As society has become more prosperous and the private sector has revolutionised the services norm, expectations are increasingly set by interactions with the private sector.

When the private sector adapts to changing circumstances, the language is very different. Commentators laud their 'innovation'; change is automatically looked upon as a good thing. The private sector changes to respond or, better still, to lead the market. If companies in the private sector do not change, they go out of business. But just because the public sector cannot 'go out of business', it does not mean that we cannot learn from the private sector. We have our market, just like business does. Our equivalent is losing the public's consent to fund progressive public services. So we need to go further in transforming the passive relationship between the citizen and the state into an active contract, with rights and greater responsibilities embedded within the system. We need to encourage a more active citizenry.

Choice is only part of the solution

Choice is not the solution to all the challenges facing public services. However, in putting choice at the forefront of reform, we have helped to transform public services. Today we are delivering a more complex and diverse range of services than ever before – from trust schools to new independent treatment and diagnostic centres – drawing on private and voluntary sector expertise across the public sector and using competition as a key driver to progress. It is not about an advanced social Darwinism or survival of the fittest, but about harnessing the potential of the market through the effective management of contestability and the creation of incentive structures that ensure that provision – no matter what its derivation – is underpinned by Labour's progressive values.

And we have made real progress. In my own constituency there has been genuine educational transformation. A decade ago the number of local children in private schools was 10.5%. Such has been the transformation in comprehensive schools that this year only 1.5% of newly enrolled pupils went to private schools. Nationally, there are now 5,800 additional good or excellent primary and secondary schools today than in 1997. Exam results are at record levels and more young people are going to university. The biggest-ever NHS hospital building programme is underway; record numbers of doctors and nurses are treating record numbers of NHS patients; deaths from cancer and heart disease are falling. Waiting lists have fallen by almost 400,000; maximum waiting times for operations have been halved from eighteen months in 1997 to nine months in April 2004, and now virtually no one waits longer than six months, with the average much lower.

But in a rapidly changing society – one facing new challenges of economic and demographic change – we have to go much further in the next decade. Many people now expect to get the best products from around the world at the touch of a button. They expect that same level of service from the public sector. Too often we seek to contextualise today's public services with those of 1997, but increasingly the public compares the responsiveness of their public services not with what happened under the Tories but with their experiences of the best in today's private sector.

Public servants – friends not foe

To retain electoral consent, taxpayers need to sense that public services are continuing to improve. Apart from personal experience, the greatest impact on public perception is the attitudes of people who work in the services. Yet we have at times been amateurish in our engagement with public servants. In the early days of New Labour this was, perhaps, understandable as we sought to prove that we were not captured by 'producer interests' or trade unions, and that we would govern for the nation and not for any one sectional interest. But in achieving this too many teachers, nurses and other public servants wrongly felt that we believed that they were part of the problem. In our communications we have relied on those who score poorest on the trust index, including ministers (22%), journalists (19%), managers (35%), trade union officials (41%) and business leaders (31%). We have not engaged enough with those who rate highly on the trust index, such as teachers (88%), police (61%) and doctors (92%).[6]

A decade later we need greater subtlety in our relationship and communications with public servants. Of course reform will continue to pick up pace, but we need to take more people with us. Such an approach is crucial as we enter an era of more autonomy and less micro-management of national targets. Public servants also want improvement, not least because they are also taxpayers and customers of the services. A start would be a proper conversation about why we need change. Too often all that people hear is the 'what' of the change, without being involved in a conversation about the 'why'. The debate is about process instead of purpose. We also need effective and direct two-way communications, which are more than a "thank you for your feedback, the contents of which have been noted". Dialogue about 'why' further changes are essential also creates challenges for trade unions and others.

An end to the politics of charity

If we are to continue to make real progress we need to reframe the debate on poverty. We should also reflect on whether government should approach poverty differently. In the past we sometimes spoke of the politics of aspiration as though it was distinct from the politics of poverty, but the politics of aspira-

6 Ipsos MORI, *Opinion of the Professions*, (Ipsos MORI, 2006), (available online at: http://www.ipsos-mori.com/trust/truth.shtml).

7 S Leitch, *The Leitch Review of Skills: Prosperity for all in the global economy – world-class skills* (HMSO, 2006).

tion and the politics of poverty are two sides of the same coin. No one aspires for change more than many people from the poorest families trapped in the poorest areas and sometimes served by poorer quality public services.

There has been real and significant progress in tackling poverty in our society. Since 1997 we have lifted 700,000 children and one million pensioners out of relative poverty. There are one million fewer people on benefits and 2.5 million more in work. And we have achieved growth with fairness. Between 1979 and 1997 inequality in the UK rose faster and went further than in any other major economy. But since 1997, growth has been more fairly shared – with incomes growing strongly for all groups, but with the poorest two-fifths actually seeing larger proportional increases than others.

Despite this improvement, entrenched pockets of deprivation still undermine the progress we have made. We have not yet managed to crack the cycle of intergenerational poverty. Inequalities in aspiration of parents drive inequalities in attainment for their children at schools.[7] The aspirations of poorer children differ from those who are better off – from the presents children ask for on their birthday, to the careers they want when they grow up. If a boy's parent is convicted of a criminal offence, he is twice as likely to be convicted himself. Relative generational mobility has fallen over time, and we are lagging behind Canada and the Nordic countries. Today we are paying the price for the policy failures of previous decades. The cycle of mobility, even at its peak, has been painfully slow.

There is a lazy analysis put forward by some commentators that because mobility has currently stalled, responsibility must lie with this administration; this assessment completely misunderstands the nature, drivers and timescales of social mobility. The time of greatest influence on an individual's social mobility is in childhood. The time of optimum influence on today's immobile 30-somethings was in the mid-1980s. Today's immobility is a legacy of the 1980s, not the past ten years.

So while New Labour did not create this decade's social immobility, we have a political and moral imperative to address it. But faced with the question 'have we done everything we can to drive future mobility?', the answer is clearly 'no, not yet'. We must focus relentlessly on improving the life chances of all children and providing second chances for adults. In particular, skills investment is essential if we are to make lasting change.

If we are to retain electoral consent for this enormous challenge we also need to reframe the debate. There has been a largely successful transformation in the language about international poverty. Over twenty years, the 'charity' of Live Aid in 1985 has been replaced by the 'self-dignity' of Live 8 in 2005. The focus has switched from charity to dignity. However, there has not been a similar change of vocabulary in the conversation about domestic poverty. The discussion about poverty in the UK is too often still about a politics of charity not a politics of aspiration. It also relentlessly focuses on a soulless conversation about government targets rather than real people.

We should also reflect on whether poverty should have a higher profile within the organisation of government. At the moment we rightly have a joined-up approach to better regulation, with a powerful cross-departmental panel for regulatory accountability, chaired by the Prime Minister. Every new bill is forensically examined for its possible impact on public sector bureaucracy or new business burden. Additional burdens are compensated for by offsetting measures. We should create a similar challenge function across government on child poverty; every policy and new bill should be examined for its impact on poverty. It is not too much to suggest that we should co-ordinate policy on child poverty as effectively as we do on unwanted paperwork.

Our methods of tackling disadvantage must also inspire aspiration. The Institute of Public Policy Research has shown that the most substantial inequalities in society are not simply between income groups, but between those who own shares, pensions and housing, and those who rely solely on wages and benefits. In the last decade the proportion of people with no assets has gone from 5% to 10%, while the value of assets, in particular housing, has grown substantially. Since 1997, household net wealth has grown by around 50% in real terms – with total household assets, including savings, pensions, life insurance and housing, standing at over £6 trillion.

Asset-based welfare must then be integral to our thinking on the way forward. The number of first-time buyers who were assisted by family and friends has grown from under 10%

8 B Duffy and R Robey, *A New British Model?* (Ipsos MORI, 2006).

in 1995 to over 40% in 2005. This illustrates the increased importance of assets. The introduction of child trust funds for all children born from September 2002 is a farsighted example of where we have already made inroads in this area. It will mean that every child has the potential to have access to a financial asset at the age of eighteen. We know that around 75% of parents have taken up this opportunity. We need to consider where this asset-based approach can be taken forward in other aspects of public services and welfare provision.

Progressive self-interest – a modern sense of social solidarity
If we are to retain the consent for our New Labour coalition, we need to reframe the debate about social justice and poverty and conceptualise it as part of a wider sense of aspiration. A modern sense of social solidarity can be based upon a renewed sense of progressive self-interest.

There is currently a democratic disconnection on domestic poverty in the UK. Only 12% of people asked in a MORI survey said that to be a good citizen, it was extremely important to support people who were worse off. Out of the twenty European countries surveyed, the UK had the second lowest tolerance threshold towards further redistribution to the poor.[8] Part of this reticence may be that when we speak about our determination to intervene to help the poorest, others perceive that we wish to place a cap on the aspirations of middle class families.

I often reflect upon my own personal experience. I grew up in one of Glasgow's poorest housing schemes and I am now the MP for the most prosperous constituency in the whole of Scotland. These two places seem worlds apart, but in truth they are separated by just one street and a mile of open ground. For me the democracy of social justice question is captured by this personal experience. How can I continue to retain the permission of those who elected me, to support those whom I grew up with? In this context, relying on traditional collective solidarity will not work. It is simply not enough if we are to secure continuing public consent for a progressive agenda. The international debate on poverty has moved on from the concept of charity, and so must we.

A different approach is also driven by electoral trends.

Fewer of those who benefit financially from Labour's focus on social justice now vote. Conversely, those who derive no immediate material advantage from Labour's determination to eradicate poverty are now an increasing proportion of those who actually vote. We should never lose focus on the electoral truism that, given demographic and turnout trends, Labour is only competitive because we have broadened our appeal. The 1964 Wilson government struggled to get a 10% share of the AB vote; in 2005 Labour achieved 28%. Those voters must remain a building block of our success.

There is also a clear connection between poverty and the decision not to vote, which, if anything, since the 1980s has become more pronounced. In the 2005 general election, over half of the 50 constituencies with the lowest voter turnout were among the 50 seats with the highest percentage of children dependent on one or more benefits, and with the highest number of people on incapacity benefit.

Progressive self-interest is about making the wider connection between personal aspiration and the continuing right of the state to enable collective solutions that meet those aspirations. It is also about re-energising the consent for Labour's values and policies. Attlee closes his autobiography by declaring his pride at living in 'the greatest country in the world.'[9] If we are to retain Attlee's civic patriotism then we need a greater intolerance of failure. In domestic policy every parent rightly wants the best for their children. Progressive self-interest encourages and celebrates that aspiration. But it also acknowledges that every child matters, and it is in all of our interests that we continue to invest in comprehensive education. The future prosperity of all our families is dependent on whether all of our citizens have the education and skills to compete.

In welfare we can't afford to have more than two and a half million people on incapacity benefit. It is a waste of human talent and affects our ability to prosper in a global economy. Perhaps more difficult to argue, but also true, is that we cannot tolerate the current levels of criminal re-offending. We should rightly consider further ways of penalising repeat offenders, but we also have to invest in rehabilitation. Four out of five prisoners have the reading ability of an eleven year old; 65% have the numeracy skills of an eleven year old; and the economic costs

9 C Attlee, *As It Happened* (Viking Adult, 1954).

alone of re-offending amount to £11 billion a year. Investment in offender skills is a crucial part of a 'tough on crime' policy. It is in all of our interests.

Internationally, progressive self-interest, at least in part, already motivates demands for action on global warming. It also bolsters the now well-established sense that if we wish to prosper in relative safety we should have a far-reaching foreign policy, which on occasion includes UK involvement in nation building. In Afghanistan, for example, the case for our continued engagement can be made by a progressive self-interest that acknowledges that 90% of heroin in the UK traditionally comes from Afghan poppy fields.

Conclusion

Aspiration created the Labour Party. If we are to retain the political and fiscal consent for Labour's values we need to continue to embrace it. This means anticipating the almost limitless aspirations of the many and lifting the near-fatalistic intergenerational poverty of aspiration of the few. We should also have a renewed confidence in eradicating poverty by transforming democratic attitudes towards domestic poverty and reframing the consent to go further. And we must not falter at the thought of further transformation of public services.

There are some who claim New Labour will wither when Tony Blair leaves Downing Street; but this ignores the nature of New Labour. It is about much more than one person. New Labour is the product of a collective and considered decision by the party as a whole in the 1990s that we wished to forge a different type of Labour Party. This remains the case.

One of New Labour's greatest political achievements is that we have repeatedly set the agenda. We must continue to do so. That agenda is one of aspiration. The challenge of our second decade is to successfully redefine the progressive sense of personal aspiration enabled through the collective capacity of the state. In doing so we can expose the bankruptcy of a Conservative philosophy of an atomised possessive individualism, which holds that aspiration can only be met by escaping from the state and public services.

Three decades ago Tony Crosland said: 'What one generation sees as a luxury, the next sees as a necessity.' Now the timeline from luxury to necessity is not a generation, but at most a decade. People's expectations and lifestyles are being transformed by technology. A decade ago mobile phones were the preserve of the more prosperous, now they are ubiquitous, with 96% of 18-24 year olds using them. In public services and politics too, the luxuries of one decade are the necessities of the next. Many radical reforms of New Labour's early years, such as devolution, disabled rights and Bank of England independence, are now the established orthodoxy of today. Many of our greatest achievements are now taken for granted. To emphasise this point, I remember talking with the assistant editor of a national newspaper about the Tory legacy of interest rates at 10% for more than four years and how we had made a decisive break from that era. I was amazed when he said: 'That's got nothing to do with what government is in power'!

This phenomenon was as true in the first days of the first Labour government as it is today. In 1924, Sidney Webb, as the President of the Board of Trade, bemoaned the fact that after only eight months in power: 'The Labour government seldom gets the credit for the very numerous works all over the country.'[10] Like Webb, we cannot expect a belated sense of gratitude from an electorate who are rightly more interested in our vision about the future than retrospection about our achievements thus far.

So, as always in politics, the past is the context. The future is the contest.

10 Labour Party, *Work for the workless: Can Labour rule?* (Labour Publications Department, 1924).

2. Poverty as an inter-generational phenomenon: bucking the trend

Dr Jo Blanden

11 Where a child is counted as poor if they are in a family that has income after housing costs below 60% of the population median – M Brewer, A Goodman, J Shaw and L Sibieta, *Poverty and Inequality in Britain* (Institute for Fiscal Studies, 2006).

At the beginning of 2006, the number of children in poverty in Britain stood at around 3.4 million,[11] which is around 27% of the child population. The fact that this many children live in relative financial hardship is a critical policy issue, and the government has committed to eradicating child poverty in the UK by 2020, although the first target of a quarter reduction in the numbers in poverty between 1998-99 and 2004-05 was narrowly missed. To help meet these targets, successive Labour governments have implemented a number of programmes to improve the incomes of families with children, including the working families tax credit and the child tax credit.

This concern about child poverty relates not just to the immediate impact of the poverty experience. The experience of poverty in childhood may influence social, economic and health outcomes in later life, leading to poverty in adulthood and consequences for the next generation. It is this intergenerational aspect of poverty that most concerns policymakers. This chapter reviews the evidence on the extent to which poverty is transmitted across generations, and offers a brief assessment of some of the reasons that poverty persists from parents to children.

I begin by reviewing the empirical work on the extent to which parents' income and poverty during an individual's childhood years affects later life chances. In particular, I measure the 'persistence of poverty' among children in the 1958 and 1970 birth cohorts; that is, the extent to which growing up in poverty increases the chances of experiencing poverty in adulthood.[12] Measuring the intergenerational transmission of income and poverty is crucial to understanding the extent to which we need to be concerned about the impact of poverty on later generations.

However, understanding the extent of the problem is of limited help in shaping an appropriate policy response. In order to determine the extent to which poverty transmissions can be tackled by redistribution, we need to know the extent to which it is low income in itself that causes difficulties for children, and the extent to which it is the other, less manipulable, characteristics of poor families that lead to later disadvantage. In the final part of the analysis described here I turn this question on its head and ask which characteristics help poor children to 'buck the trend' and avoid poverty in their own adult lives.[13]

The intergenerational transmission of income and poverty
In order to investigate the relationship between parental circumstances and children's later economic fortunes, we need data that observes children's family circumstances and then returns to see how they are doing later in life. Fortunately we can observe these pieces of information in the two British cohort studies: the national child development study and the British cohort study. The availability of these two sources of data, one a cohort born in one week in 1958 and the other a cohort born in a week in 1970, allows us to compare the fortunes of those growing up in the 1970s with those growing up poor in the 1980s.

The interest in the persistence of poverty across generations stems from a wider concern about the impact of family background on economic outcomes. A summary measure of the extent to which economic outcomes are related across generations is known as 'intergenerational persistence'; it is measured as the coefficient on parental income when regressed on children's outcomes, as in Equation 1. Conversely, the degree of independence is called 'intergenerational mobility', in general a low β is seen as indicating substantial mobility. The interpretation of β is that it tells us the proportion of any income difference between parents that is passed on to the next generation.

12 These results are taken from J Blanden and S Gibbons, *The Persistence of Poverty: A view from two British cohorts* (Joseph Rowntree, Policy Press, 2006).

13 This section is drawn from J Blanden, *Bucking the Trend: What enables those who are disadvantaged in childhood to succeed in later life?* Working Paper No 31 (Department for Work and Pensions, 2006).

14 β and *r* come from a regression of sons' earnings at age 33/30 on parental income at age 16.

Equation 1: the relationship between parental and children's incomes

$$\ln Y_i^{children} = \alpha + \beta \ln Y_i^{parents} + \varepsilon_i$$

Table 1 gives estimates of intergenerational persistence in the 1958 and 1970 cohorts. Here β is calculated from a regression of parental income at age sixteen on son's adult earnings in his early 30s, and r is the partial correlation between these two variables. For sons born in 1958, the elasticity of own earnings with respect to parental income at age sixteen was 0.205; for sons born in 1970 the elasticity was 0.291. This is a clear and statistically significant growth in the relationship between economic status across generations. For the correlation estimates, the fall in mobility is even more pronounced. The correlation for the 1958 cohort is 0.166 compared with 0.286 for the 1970 cohort.

Table 1: Changes in intergenerational mobility[14]

	1958 cohort	1970 cohort	Change
β	.205 (.026)	.291 (.025)	.086 (.036)
Partial Correlation (*r*)	.166 (.021)	.286 (.025)	.119 (.033)
Sample Size	2163	1976	

Source: J Blanden, P Gregg and L Macmillan, *Accounting for Intergenerational Income Persistence: Non-cognitive skills, ability and education, Centre for the Economics of Education Discussion Paper No. 73* (Centre for the Economics of Education, 2006), table 4.

These results for intergenerational mobility give the average relationship between parental income and later earnings across the two cohorts. They provide some evidence that the impact of growing up in disadvantage may have increased when comparing the two cohorts. However, intergenerational mobility results may not give us a correct picture on the transmission of poverty because the relationship between parental income and later outcomes is different for poor families (non-linearity), or because of non-earned income such as benefits and the partner's income (where there is one). Therefore, it is informative to look directly at poverty.

Our initial estimates of the persistence of poverty are based on comparing poverty rates in their early 30s for those who grew up in poverty compared with those who did not. Of those who were teenagers in the 1970s:

- for those whose families were poor when they were sixteen, 19% of those with poor parents are poor and 81% are not. Individuals are *four* times more likely to be non-poor than poor in their early 30s.
- for those with parents who are not poor, 90% are not poor in later life while 10% are poor. In this case, individuals are *nine* times more likely to be non-poor than poor if their parents were non-poor.

Persistence is measured by comparing these two numbers, the chances (or odds) of being poor if one's parents are poor with the chances of being poor if they are not (the odds ratio).

Calculations of the odds ratio find that, for those who were teenagers in the 1970s, poverty at sixteen doubled the odds of being poor as an adult. Similar calculations for the later cohort who were teenagers in the 1980s show that the odds of being poor in adulthood were nearly quadrupled by having poor parents (see Figure 1). Comparing these odds across the cohorts indicates that the strength of poverty persistence has approximately doubled, with an increase for men that is slightly greater than the rise for women.

15 Data from the British Cohort Study (BCS) and the National Child Development Study (NCDS). The bars report the odds ratios for poverty at sixteen in a logit model of poverty at age 33 for the earlier cohort and age 30 for the later cohort. Vertical scale is in logarithms.

Figure 1: How teenage poverty affects the odds of being poor as an adult[15]

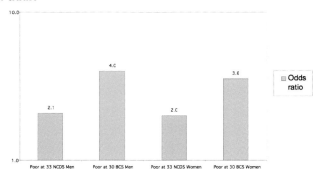

Source: J Blanden and S Gibbons, *The Persistence of Poverty across Generations* (Policy Press, 2006), fig. 2.

Suggestive evidence on how poverty is transmitted
These results indicate that child poverty has an association with poverty at later ages, and that this association is stronger among the 1970 cohort. The important policy question these results encourage us to ask is – what is it about growing up in poverty that makes it more likely that poor children will experience disadvantage in later life? This is crucial in terms of putting in place effective policies to alleviate the impacts of early disadvantage. For example, if we can show that it is lack of money in itself that is causing children to do badly then redistribution is an obvious solution, and reducing child poverty through benefits will have important impacts.

We know that poor families differ in many ways to those who are not poor: they are more likely to be headed by parents who have low education, less employment and those who are lone parents. Policy prescriptions are more difficult if it is these factors that lead to poorer outcomes for children, as they are much less subject to change. The datasets used here include information on family characteristics, enabling us to measure the extent to which they are connected with poverty in later life.

To understand the extent to which observable characteristics can account for the transmission of poverty across generations we can use regression techniques to calculate the odds ratios conditional on these variables. That is, we show the association between poverty across generations, holding parental characteristics constant.

Results from this exercise are shown in Figure 2, which compares the odds ratios with and without controls for parental characteristics. For the teenagers growing up in the 1970s, it seems that the impact of these factors on children can explain all of the higher poverty rates for children who experienced poverty as teenagers. It was their family characteristics, in particular, their parents' poor education and lack of work that resulted in their later poverty and not the fact that their parents lacked income per se. For those who were teenagers in the 1980s this is not the case. Even when taking account of family characteristics there is evidence that poverty in itself puts these young people at a significant disadvantage.

Figure 2: Intergenerational poverty links controlling for parental characteristics[16]

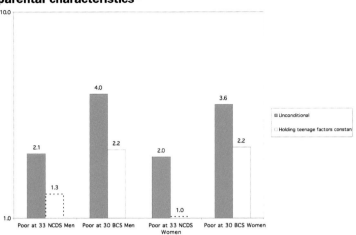

16 Data from the British Cohort Study (BCS) and the National Child Development Study (NCDS). The bars report the odds ratios for poverty at sixteen in a logit model of poverty at age 33 for the earlier cohort and age 30 for the later cohort. Vertical scale is in logarithms. The first bar in each pair is the unconditional odds ratio while the second bar conditions on lone parent family at sixteen, number of children in the household, parental education, parental employment and the child's health. Dotted lines surrounding the bar indicate an insignificant relationship.

Source: Based on J Blanden, and S Gibbons, *The Persistence of Poverty across Generations* (Policy Press, 2006), fig. 3.

This result can be taken to imply that straightforward redistribution would have had substantial benefits for the younger group. However, this conclusion is too simplistic as it does not take account of the ways in which poor and non-poor families differ that are difficult to observe. For example, we do not have a measure of the parents' ability to help and encourage their children to learn and persevere. In the final section of this chapter I present evidence that attempts to exploit the richness of the 1970 cohort to identify the characteristics that appear to help children avoid poverty later in life.

The characteristics that help children 'buck the trend'

Our analysis so far has demonstrated a clear link between poverty across the lifecycle; however, the majority of children who experience child poverty avoid adult poverty at age 30. Consequently the idea of 'bucking the trend' is somewhat of a misnomer, but in this final section I compare the characteristics of those children in the 1970 cohort who avoid poverty with those for whom disadvantage continues in later life.

The policy relevance of considering this question is

extremely clear: identifying the characteristics of those who avoid poverty may help government to design policies to help children in disadvantage achieve their maximum potential, and avoid the cycle of disadvantage identified above. However, we must bear in mind that identifying a link between characteristics may not indicate that a policy focused on these characteristics would be successful. For example, if we find that children do better if they are taken to museums, a policy to encourage school trips to museums will not necessarily help children if this variable is actually a proxy for parents' overall enthusiasm for education. One of the benefits of using the 1970 cohort is the richness of the dataset, meaning that not only do we have lots of potential candidates for the characteristics that help children 'buck the trend', but also that we can control for the importance of other variables, making it less likely that different influences are confounded.

In my research I concentrate on those aspects of children's experience that are connected with educational attainment, as this is seen by many as a key route through which children can escape a poor start in life. Initial results in the first panel of Table 2 indicate very clearly that children who escape poverty are generally those who achieve higher qualifications. This investigation takes the next step, moving beyond the observation of the result that children who do well at school are more likely to 'buck the trend' and look more closely at *why* some children manage to do well.

Specifically, I chose to investigate two broad areas: parents' attitudes to learning and the peer group children experience at school. To proxy parental attitudes I use the parents' answers to the question, 'How many times has X been read to in the last week?' in the age five questionnaire, and the teacher's report of each parent's interest in the child's education in the age ten questionnaire. Peer group is modelled by the child's headteacher's responses to questions about the ability and socioeconomic mix of the children in the school at age ten.

The analysis in the second panel of Table 2 makes it clear that considerably more of those children who 'buck the trend' had parents who took a strong interest in their education and who read to them. For example, almost 30% of those who were poor at age 30 were not read to during the survey week, compared to 15% of those who go on to buck the trend. The results from the school analysis indicate that children who bucked the trend tend to go to school with a lower proportion of low ability children compared to those whose early disadvantage persists. The lower panel shows that there is also an association between later poverty and going to school with few children from higher social backgrounds. The descriptive results, therefore, indicate that effective policies to help poor children would promote parental engagement and emphasise the importance of mixed schooling (i.e. avoiding concentrating poor children in schools with high numbers of socially disadvantaged or less able students).

However, the interpretation drawn from these comparisons may be overly simplistic. It could be that these variables are simply picking up other differences among children and their parents. The apparent importance of reading to children may simply be picking up the fact that the more highly educated parents are those who tend to read to their children. Similarly, the findings on peer ability may simply be reflecting the sorting of children into schools; those children who attend schools with fewer low ability children are more able themselves and therefore more likely to 'buck the trend'.

We can never fully resolve these issues, but using some additional variables in multivariate analyses does allow them to be investigated. Detailed information on parental education and social class can be used to explore whether differences in parents behaviour along these dimensions drives the results found so far. Children's ability at ages five and ten was measured using a number of age-appropriate tests. This can help understand the relationship between parental interest and the child's ability, and also clarify how children of differing abilities sort into schools.

The results from the multivariate analysis differ from the descriptive findings in a number of ways. Table 3 reveals that there is no evidence that reading to children has a particular benefit, as this appears to be a proxy for parental interest in education. Indeed, parental interest is very important in helping children buck the trend, and shows up in all our models. The multivariate results reveal some interesting differences in these variables between girls and boys. For boys, father's interest is particularly important in helping them escape disadvantage, while for girls, mother's influence dominates. For a boy, having a father who is very interested in his education rather than one with little interest increases the chances of him avoiding poverty by 30 percentage points. The negative impact of having a mother with no interest in her daughter's education is even larger.

The other variable found to be important in helping children escape poverty is the ability mix of the child's school. In the multivariate analysis (not shown here) it seems that being educated with more above-average ability children benefits poor boys. There is no impact for girls. It does not appear that the effect for boys is picking up the boys' own ability, as the results are not affected when ability is controlled for. However, it is possible that unobserved differences remain between boys who attend different types of school.

Concluding remarks

This article has reviewed recent results from several studies of the impact of poverty on children's development and future life chances. It is clear that children who grow up in poverty face a substantially higher risk of being disadvantaged adults, and that this association increased between a cohort growing up in the 1970s and one growing up in the 1980s. For the second cohort the intergenerational association in poverty cannot be accounted for by simple differences between parental education, employment and family structure among poor and non-poor families.

While it is clear that children who grow up in poverty are more likely to be poor as adults, this relationship is by no means deterministic. Indeed, most children who grow up in poverty do not grow up to be poor adults. I have therefore looked for those factors in early childhood that may help children avoid poverty later on. There is evidence that strong achievement on age five test scores and parental interest in education can help children escape the cycle of disadvantage.

Although these findings do not provide governments with a 'quick fix' to help poor children, there is a suggestion here that policies focused on supporting parents and young children might have benefits. Recent policies, such as Sure Start, are clearly moving in this direction. However, designing policy to successfully influence parenting behaviour is extremely difficult, and it is crucial that interventions such as Sure Start are properly evaluated to ensure that policy is as effective as possible in helping poor children fulfil their potential and escape the cycle of poverty. The current early evidence from the National Evaluation of Sure Start Team[17] has not yet been able to identify any beneficial effects on children's test scores, although there is some evidence of more supportive and accepting parenting from mothers. As the evaluation proceeds and the children age we shall be able to see if this translates into more interest in the child's schooling or other positive outcomes that will help poor kids to avoid an intergenerational cycle of disadvantage.

17 National Evaluation of Sure Start Team, *Early Impacts of Sure Start Local Programmes on Children and Families: Research paper no. 13* (National Evaluation of Sure Start, 2005).

Table 2: Differences between children who "buck the trend" and those who do not

Sample is all those poor at 16 where this is defined as if their income is below the poverty line in the FES data for 1986.

	Poor at 30	Not poor at 30	Difference (standard error)
Education outcomes			
Low education at age 16	.447	.289	.157 (.043)
Number of O levels/good CSEs at 16	1.615	3.251	-1.635 (.344)
Highest educational qualification at age 30 (0-8 scale)	2.607	4.076	-1.468 (.189)
Parental interest and reading behaviour			
The child was not read to during the survey week (age 5)	.288	.149	.140 (.033)
Father very interested in child's education (age 10)	.077	.237	-.159 (.034)
Mother very interested in child's education (age 10)	.175	.402	-.227 (.040)
Age 10 peer group			
Relatively few low ability children in child's school (<3%)	.138	.200	-.062 (.032)
Relatively many low ability children in child's school (>10%)	.530	.427	.103 (.041)
Relatively few children with professional parents in child's school (<2%)	.335	.267	.068 (.037)

Table 3: Multivariate analysis of characteristics associated with "bucking the trend"

Parental interest and reading behaviour	Boys	Girls
The child was not read to during the survey week (age 5)	-.123 (.073)	-.117 (.070)
The child was read to once or twice during the survey week	-.092 (.065)	.053 (.056)
The child was read to three to six times	.002 (.052)	.017 (.051)
Father moderate interest in child's education	-.128 (.095)	.078 (.071)
Father little interest in child's education	-.317 (.155)	-.103 (.133)
Father no interest in child's education	-.152 (.165)	-.114 (.090)
Teacher cannot comment on father's interest	-.176 (.086)	-.083 (.076)
Mother moderate interest in child's education	-.091 (.060)	-.199 (.067)
Mother little interest in child's education	-.032 (.093)	-.139 (.109)
Mother no interest in child's education	-.079 (.143)	-.576 (.138)
Teacher cannot comment on mother's interest	-.059 (.071)	-.163 (.080)
Number of individuals in the sample	530	586

Source: Author's calculations from British Cohort Study; some numbers also appear in Tables 4.1, 4.2 and 4.3 of J Blanden, *Bucking the Trend: What enables those who are disadvantaged in childhood to succeed in later life?*, Working Paper No 31 (Department for Work and Pensions, 2006).

3. Child poverty: avoiding a life sentence

Lisa Harker

The fact that our country has such a high level of child poverty often comes as something of a surprise. The UK has a strong economy and the highest employment rate among the G8 member countries. Living standards are good and continue to improve. In many ways children's lives are more enriched than ever.

But changes that took place during the 1980s, when the gap between rich and poor rose faster in the UK than in almost any other industrialised country, are still reflected in the shape of our society today. During that period child poverty rates tripled, as the incomes of the poorest failed to keep up with the rest of society. By the early 1990s one in three children were living in relative poverty. Those children who grew up in poverty in the 1980s are, as Jo Blanden explains in Chapter 2, also more likely to be living in poverty today. The pulling apart of society in the late twentieth century has left a devastating legacy.

Child poverty levels have fallen since the mid 1990s, largely as a consequence of the government's determination to eradicate child poverty in a generation. The Prime Minister's 1999 pledge to end child poverty by 2020 paved the way for a series of policy reforms that have substantially improved the level of support provided to families with children. As a result of changes to the tax and benefit system and the introduction of a national minimum wage, the poorest families with children are, on average, £3,350 a year better off.[18] Welfare to work programmes have enabled more parents to move into work. The

18 This relates to the poorest 20% of families.

19 This is calculated by measuring the number of children living in families on incomes below 60% of the median. The child poverty rate is 19% when using a before-housing costs measure and 27% when using an after-housing costs measure.

20 N Spencer, *Poverty and Child Health* (Radcliffe, 2nd edition, 2000).

21 P Gregg, S Harkness and S Machin, *Child Development and Family Income* (Joseph Rowntree Foundation, 1999); A McCulloch and H E Joshi , *Child Development and Family Resources: An exploration of evidence from the second generation of the 1958 British birth cohort* (Institute for Social and Economic Research Working Paper, University of Essex, 1999); J Bradshaw, *Poverty: The outcomes for children* (Family Policy Studies Centre, 2001); J Ermisch, F Francesconi and D Pevalin, *Outcomes for Children of Poverty: Department for Work and Pensions Research Report 158* (Institute for Social and Economic Research, 2001).

22 L Harker, *Chance of a Lifetime* (Shelter, 2006).

impact has been significant: the number of children in poverty has decreased by 700,000 since 1998. The child poverty rate is now at a fifteen-year low and the UK no longer has the highest child poverty rate in the European Union.

But the progress has not been sufficient to reach the government's interim target to reduce child poverty by 25% by 2005. Around one in five children still live in poverty.[19] Income inequality remains high, driven by high levels of wage and wealth inequality. The benefits of our rich society – in the distribution of income and employment opportunities – are not being evenly shared.

The impact is evident across nearly every indicator of health, social and economic wellbeing. Children born into low income families are more likely to be of a low birth weight (which is itself a health risk), die in the first year of life, and suffer significant episodes of illness.[20] They are also more likely than their better-off peers to have low educational attainment, leave school at sixteen, come into early contact with police, be unemployed as young adults, have low expectations for the future, and end up earning a relatively low wage.[21]

The impact of poverty on a child's life begins even before birth: having an insufficient income can limit a mother's diet during pregnancy, which affects a child's development. Poverty also restricts a family's ability to participate in everyday activities, limiting aspirations as well as opportunities. It can mean living in an environment so damp or cold that it has an immediate and long-term damaging influence on children's health and general wellbeing.[22] It can result in living in the constant shadow of debt. And it can have a detrimental impact on parents' emotional wellbeing, which, in turn, can affect a child's development: parental depression is strongly linked to children's behavioural problems and low levels of educational attainment.

Of course, the associations between poverty and children's life chances are in no sense deterministic. Many children who grow up in poverty do not experience health, behavioural, learning or emotional problems later in life. But the risk of damaged life chances is heightened, particularly when poverty is experienced in the early years. Indeed, growing up in poverty remains one of the most powerful predictors of later life chances.

The impact of child poverty is devastating in personal terms, but it also affects wider society. The costs to society of lost opportunities, ill health and unemployment are obvious. High levels of child poverty also explain the UK's comparatively poor record on child welfare – the UK has relatively high levels of low birth weight babies, infant mortality, poor child health and high levels of risky behaviour (teenage pregnancy, drug and alcohol misuse) among young people[23] compared with other European Union countries.

None of this has escaped the attention of the current government, which has sought to transform support for families with children. Its child poverty strategy, as set out in the government's 2004 *Child Poverty Review,* has been to improve financial support for families, help parents into employment, reform public services to enhance children's life chances, and support parents in their parenting role. Increases to tax credits and benefits for families have played an important role in tackling child poverty. Welfare-to-work programmes have also made a difference by helping more parents into employment. There has been an increase of eleven percentage points in the lone parent employment rate since 1997, for example.

In the longer term, changes to children's services through the Every Child Matters reforms and development of new services, such as Sure Start local programmes and children's centres, are likely to have a significant impact on child poverty. Indeed, if they are successful in countering disadvantage and breaking the generational link between poverty and children's life chances, these reforms will prove to be the most significant of all.

But important as all these changes have been, they will not be sufficient to meet the government's goal to eradicate child poverty. On current policies child poverty is not expected to fall significantly: unless there is further change the government will miss its next target of halving child poverty by 2010, and stand no chance of eradicating child poverty by 2020.

Work undertaken for the Joseph Rowntree Foundation[24] has estimated that the 2010 target could be met if a further £4.3 billion per annum were invested in benefits and tax credits. But an effective anti-poverty strategy must invest in people's capabilities and widen their opportunities, as well as providing a better safety net. For many families an income through paid

23 J Bradshaw, P Hoelscher and D Richardson, *An Index of Child-wellbeing in the European Union* (Social Indicators Research, 2006).

24 D Hirsch, *What Would it Take to End Child Poverty? Firing on all cylinders* (Joseph Rowntree Foundation, 2006).

25 L Harker, *Delivering on Child Poverty: What would it take?; Command Paper 6951* (Department for Work and Pensions, 2006).

employment offers a more effective and sustainable route out of poverty. While the government has already placed much emphasis on welfare-to-work policies within its strategy to tackle child poverty, there are strong grounds for believing that parental employment rates could continue to rise beyond current levels. Lone parent employment rates are low by European Union standards, and while 69% of all couple families where someone is work are dual earning, only 24% of poor couples where someone is in work are dual earners. The most effective way of tackling child poverty is for parental employment rates to rise, together with an increase in financial support.

To help more parents into employment changes are necessary,[25] however. Welfare-to-work support needs to be more attuned to the particular needs of parents, to take account of the increasing involvement of fathers in children's lives, the converging aspirations of men and women in the labour market and the juggling of work and family commitments, which many parents negotiate daily. Welfare-to-work programmes also need to move beyond a simple 'work-first' approach: to thrive in today's rapidly changing labour market parents need guidance, support and skills to progress in work. And there will be a need to extend the reach of support to help, for example, potential second earners in a family to find work.

While such changes could make a significant difference to child poverty levels, they will not be sufficient to reduce child poverty levels in the UK to among the lowest in Europe. Despite a substantial increase in financial support for families, rising levels of employment among parents and new services, such as Sure Start, which have all made a difference, we have yet to witness the scale of change needed to tackle the intergenerational transmission of disadvantage and poverty.

What would it take to reduce child poverty radically? Three issues immediately present themselves: the need to increase the transformative nature of education, to tackle wider inequalities in society, and to achieve a public mandate for change.

Closing the education divide

Despite the evidence that educational attainment can help children escape a life in poverty, social background remains a stronger predictor of achievement in the UK than in many other countries. Breaking the link between educational achievement and intergenerational poverty will be key to making long-term progress on child poverty.

While the proportion of children achieving five GCSEs at grade A* to C in England has increased by more than ten percentage points in the last decade, children from poorer backgrounds are still less likely to gain higher grade qualifications than their better-off peers – a divergence in attainment that cannot be explained on the grounds of differing ability. This educational divide starts young: research has identified a fourteen percentage point difference in cognitive development between children from social classes I and II compared to those from social classes IV and V by the age of 22 months.[26] It points to the need to support parenting and high quality early years' services, which have been shown to benefit particularly children from disadvantaged families.[27] Encouraging parents' involvement in their children's learning is also key, since this is one of the strongest predictors of a child's chances of escaping poverty.[28] Support for pre-school children is improving with the roll-out of children's centres, the expansion in childcare services and increased investment in parenting support. But the government needs to ensure that there is greater take-up of such support among the most disadvantaged, who are still least likely to benefit from such services, and that the quality of early years' support is sufficiently high to make a difference.

Tackling educational inequalities also requires the positive impact of pre-school education to be maintained. In recent years, while schools with more deprived pupils have generally seen their average results improve faster than schools with less deprived pupils, the attainment of the poorest pupils has improved more slowly than their peers.

The government's 2004 *Child Poverty Review* rightly pointed to the need to examine the level of funding received by schools in disadvantaged areas. Additional funding for such schools could be invested in attracting the best teachers and reducing class sizes, both would have a particularly beneficial impact on disadvantaged pupils. But overall much greater attention needs to be paid generally to the policies and practices that can help disadvantaged pupils thrive at school, and the Department for Education and Skills should set targets to reduce inequalities in

26 L Feinstein, *Pre-school Educational Inequality?* (Centre for Economic Performance, London School of Economics, 1998).

27 K Sylva, I Siraj-Blatchford, B Taggart, P Sammons, E Melhuish and K Elliot, *The Effective Provision of Pre-School Education (EPPE) Project: Findings from the pre-school period* (IOE, 2003).

28 Blanden, (2006), op.cit.

individual attainment as well as inequalities between advantaged and disadvantaged areas.

Improving education and skills will be critical to ensuring that tomorrow's parents thrive in the labour market. Although a parent's skills and qualifications are a key determinant of their income, and therefore their chances of escaping poverty, the government's child poverty strategy has placed little emphasis on skills acquisition to date. However, Lord Leitch's review of skills for government has made a clear case for greater investment in adult skills to help tackle child poverty.[29]

Unless skill levels increase rapidly among those on low incomes, progress towards eradicating child poverty will be slow. There is expected to be a 25% decline in demand for unskilled labour by 2010. While the demand for highly skilled workers will continue to outpace the decline in low skilled jobs, in an economy where five million working age adults lack any qualifications it will become increasingly difficult to match supply with demand. A generation of workers could find themselves permanently excluded from the labour market, heightening their risk of poverty and that of their children. Supporting parents to find a job will not be sufficient – they also need help with gaining skills to ensure that they advance in work.

Tackling wider inequality

With a rising level of median income, driven by fast but unequal growth in income, assets and wages, it is not easy to make progress on child poverty. Between 1996 and 2001, income inequality rose to its highest level since comparable records began in 1961. Income inequality has since fallen back to roughly the level that Labour inherited. But it is still less likely now that an individual will escape poverty in his or her lifetime than 30 years ago. Progress on child poverty will be held back unless it is possible to share the rewards of the UK's prosperity more equally.

The government has sought to address some of these inequalities by, among other things, improving benefit levels for families with children, widening access to savings schemes, extending opportunities for home ownership and improving wage levels through the introduction of the minimum wage and in-work tax credits. These steps to redistribute income and opportunities have had a clear impact on child poverty. But to make further progress, much further inroads need to be made into tackling income and wealth inequality. Far greater changes to the distribution of wealth, earnings and opportunities in society are needed – to ensure all are aboard the moving caravan, to evoke Polly Toynbee's much-quoted analogy – in order for child poverty to be significantly reduced.

The government has been timid about having an overt strategy to reduce inequality, preferring to undertake redistribution by stealth. Yet surveys have found that citizens accept inequality based on talent, effort or even luck, but that they also believe the ratio of wealth between the poorest and the richest should be of the order of around 25 to one. In fact the ratio between the top 5000 people in Britain and the poor is more like 500 to one.

Britain's wage distribution bears little resemblance to the widely held notion of fairness. The average total pay for chief executives of the FTSE 100 companies increased by more than 40% in the past year, while wage settlements ran at around 3%.[30] Chief executives in the biggest UK companies now earn 98 times more than the average of all full-time UK employees – whereas twenty years ago the ratio of chief executive pay to the average was closer to nine to one. And while this pulling away of the richest 1% or so of the population has little direct impact on child poverty levels (which are measured against median income), it nevertheless threatens to fracture a society and undermine a sense of mutual endeavour towards achieving a fairer nation. Such inequalities cannot be explained by market forces or the exceptional nature of the UK's top executives. Other successful economies do not share our wage distribution. A fairer distribution of income, wealth and opportunities is within our grasp.

Establishing a public mandate for change

However, in the absence of public support for greater intervention, the government's options look very constrained indeed.

Although child poverty is one of the government's most important priorities, and a broader political consensus about the importance of reducing child poverty has recently emerged, the issue barely registers on the public's agenda. Nor is there much

30 Income Data Services, *Directors' Pay Report* (Income Data Services, 2006).

31 Fabian Society, *Narrowing the Gap: The final report of the Fabian Commission on Life Chances and Child Poverty* (Fabian Society, 2006).

awareness of the progress that has been made to date, or the scale of the task that lies ahead. Fewer people believe poverty to be a serious problem in Britain today than a decade ago. And while the majority of the public thinks that the gap between those on high and low incomes is too wide, many people are wary of government intervention to tackle poverty and inequality. Research conducted by the Fabian Society has shown that people often attribute poverty to individual failings, such as laziness or an inability to parent effectively, rather than simply a lack of material resources.[31] It will be hard for any government to gain support for its child poverty goals simply on the basis of sympathy for those who are worst affected.

Raising awareness about child poverty in the UK is a challenge that policymakers and campaign groups share. There is little doubt that opaque measurement of child poverty fails to resonate with the public: it should come as no surprise that the need to reduce the number of children living in households on incomes below 60% of the median after housing costs has yet to become a rallying cry. Such language tends to be alienating. Talk of improving 'social mobility' or 'building a progressive consensus' does not resonate far beyond academe or the Westminster village. A more open and inclusive dialogue needs to describe the kind of society that we wish to build, if hearts and minds are to be won over. And the extent and nature of child poverty in Britain will only become clear when it is told in stories that fit with people's own everyday experiences.

There is also a need to confront misguided attitudes to poverty, to demonstrate that while someone living in poverty is not absolved of any personal responsibility for their situation, discrimination, unequal opportunities and bad luck can also play a part. Outdated notions of poverty also need to be challenged. There remains a tendency to present 21st century child poverty in Victorian imagery of rags and starvation. That nearly half of children living in poverty now live in a family where someone is in work underlines the fact that, for the most part, poverty is no longer a question of being destitute but of being left behind by a society that is failing to share its riches fairly.

In presenting these issues to the public there is a need to strike a balance between making the self-interest case for tackling child poverty – setting out how a reduction in child poverty could benefit society as a whole – and the moral case, which will help to bind commitment to tackling child poverty, whatever the circumstances. Similarly, the action that government takes must chime with the public's sense of fairness. A strategy that fails to encourage people to take some responsibility for their destiny is unlikely to attract public support.

Tackling child poverty remains one of the most important missions of our time. It reflects not only a desire to transform the life chances of a generation of children, but also an ambition to build a fairer, more equal society. But while policymakers debate the respective responsibilities of individuals, employers, government and wider society in this endeavour, the public appear yet to be convinced of the scale of the problem. In the absence of public support for increased action, it will be difficult to do more than continue on the current course, which will not be sufficient to reduce child poverty significantly. Without a public mandate for further change, we may already be very near the limits of what can be achieved.

4. Access to education and basic skills: the first step on the ladder of achievement

32 J Blanden, P Gregg and L Macmillan, 'Accounting for intergenerational income persistence: Non cognitive skills, ability and education' (*The Economic Journal*, forthcoming 2007).

33 M Jäntti, B Bratsberg, K Røed, O Raaum, R Naylor, E Osterbacka,, A Bjorklund and T Eriksson, *American Exceptionalism in a New Light: A comparison of intergenerational earnings mobility in the Nordic countries, the United Kingdom and the United States, Discussion Paper No. 1938,* (IZA, 2006); M Corak, *Do Poor Children Become Poor Adults? Lessons from a cross country comparison of generational earnings mobility, Discussion paper No. 1993* (IZA, 2006).

34 J Blanden, A Goodman, P Gregg and S Machin, 'Changes in intergenerational mobility in Britain' in M Corak, (ed), *Generational Income Mobility in North America and Europe* (Cambridge University Press, 2004).

35 Op.cit., ref. 32.

Professor Paul Gregg and Lindsey Macmillan

A key measure of an individual's life chances is the level of inter-generational income mobility within a country. If mobility is low, those who grow up in poor families are more likely to end up in poor families as adults. If mobility is high, those from poor families have a greater chance of leaving this group and earning higher wages in adulthood, and hence have greater life chances. This essay discusses recent findings by Blanden, Gregg and Macmillan[32] on the interactions that occur that lead family background to influence life chances, with a particular focus on the role of skills, education and early labour market attachment in determining later outcomes.

There have been two main focuses of recent research in this area: international comparisons of mobility, and changes in mobility within the UK across time. The main findings of this are that the level of mobility in the UK is low by international standards,[33] and that the extent of mobility in the UK fell when considering two British birth cohorts, children born in a week in March 1958 and April 1970.[34] With the idea that individuals' life chances should not be determined by birth an important political notion, it is thus important to try to understand why mobility is so low in the UK, and what has led to this decrease in mobility across time.

Recent research by Blanden, Gregg and Macmillan[35] attempts to account for the key mediating influences in the strong relationship between family income in childhood and adult earnings. The first stage of this process attempts to account for the low level of mobility in the UK by examining the role played by four components – education, cognitive ability, non-cognitive traits, and labour market attachment – in this transmission of parents' income to adult earnings, using the cohort of children born in 1970. The second stage considers the changing nature of the relationship between these four components, parents' income and adult earnings, using the 1958 and 1970 cohorts, in an attempt to account for the decrease in mobility across time.

The evidence suggests that personal skills, including cognitive ability and non-cognitive traits, education and early labour market attachment, can account for over half of the intergenerational persistence in incomes in the 1970 cohort, with inequalities in educational attainment at sixteen, access to further education and early labour market attachment playing key roles in this. When considering the decrease in mobility across time, the findings suggest that up to 90% of the decrease in mobility can be accounted for, with the increase in the relationship of parents' income with education and early labour market attachment accounting for much of the action. Importantly, the research suggests there is no substantive role for innate ability behind the decline in mobility, but that non-cognitive traits, such as 'application', self-esteem and personal efficacy, do contribute to the decline in mobility. In other words, poor children's education and life chances fell further behind those from affluent families, but this was not due to underlying ability. This finding highlights the importance of educational attainment at age sixteen, the skills that influence this attainment, and the decisions to pursue education thereafter. It also suggests that policymakers should be concerned about the continuing high number of NEETs (those not in education, employment or training) among Britain's youth. This group have very poor life chances according to research using the birth cohorts, discussed later.

What are the main drivers of low levels of mobility in the UK?
In this research we focus on the role of five components or groupings of variables in describing the patterns of intergenera-

36 Measured by the regression coefficient of son's earnings on parental income with controls for parents' age, gender of the child and employment status at 30.

37 Mobility is thought of as $(1-\beta)$ where β is the regression coefficient of intergenerational persistence.

tional mobility we observe. These are cognitive ability before age ten, non-cognitive traits before age ten, educational attainment at age sixteen, educational attainment after age sixteen, and attachment to the labour market after leaving full-time education. To analyse the role each component plays in the transmission of parents' income to earnings, the intergenerational persistence coefficient[36] can be decomposed. The larger this coefficient, the higher the persistence, or the lower the level of mobility.[37] For the components in question to account for mobility there are two conditions: first they must have a relationship with family income, and second they must have a return in the labour market. Therefore a simple two-stage process is used: first, by measuring the extent to which a component is related to parents' income, and second, by estimating the returns these components will have in the labour market. The product of these two measurements reflects the extent to which a component can account for the level of persistence.

As the model contains components measured at different stages in a child's life, components that are measured earlier in the child's life may well affect later components. So, for example, the individual's educational attainment at sixteen will impact on the level of earnings at 30 obtained directly, but also through their early labour market experiences, as those who have poor attainment are more likely to experience early detachment from the labour market. Likewise, innate ability will undoubtedly impact on educational attainment, and its effect on future earnings will, to some degree, come through educational attainment. Therefore, to explore these sequential effects the model is built up in stages over periods of time. The results from using the 1970 cohort indicate that all four major components considered (cognitive and non-cognitive attainment at ages five and ten, educational attainment and labour market attachment) are important in accounting for the high levels of intergenerational persistence.

All of the components in question have significant relationships with parents' income, fulfilling the first condition for them to play a role in accounting for the high levels of persistence. When considering the second condition, whether the components have a return to earnings, the sequential nature of the model tells a number of stories. The role of cognitive ability and non-cognitive traits diminishes once the age sixteen educational attainments are included, suggesting that both of these childhood measurements influence earnings through education. The most strongly affected measure is the child's application score at age ten. Children who are observed with a score substantially above the average level of application (a 1 standard deviation increase) earn an extra 4.7% as adults, but this is almost entirely achieved through higher educational attainment. This suggests that children who apply themselves more at the age of ten are receiving higher earnings through the achievement of more O levels at grades A-C.

The estimated additional earnings for one more O level (now GCSE grades A-C) at age sixteen are 3.6% at age 30. Likewise, with the inclusion of post-sixteen education we can see that half these returns to age sixteen attainment come through opening access to higher education. When the number of A levels achieved, whether the individual stays on post-sixteen and the achievement of a degree are included, the coefficient for the returns to the number of O levels diminishes by a half. The coefficients on the early childhood scores are unaffected, suggesting that higher cognitive and non-cognitive scores in childhood do not predict the likelihood of staying on in education post-sixteen. The additional returns to achieving a degree, given the number of O levels and A levels achieved, are 15% additional earnings at age 30.

The attachment to the labour market in early adulthood also has a large influence on the earnings of the sons at 30, and therefore plays another important role in accounting for the high level of intergenerational persistence in the UK. Of the quarter of the sample that experience some time in unemployment, these men can expect to have on average 12% lower wages than those who experience no unemployment, and on average are unemployed for 10% of the period between the completion of full-time education and the age of 30 (around nineteen months). Other research suggests this is causal, such that youth unemployment damages future earnings rather than reflecting any other unobserved characteristics of these youths.[38]

To consider the whole story of the extent to which each component can account for the high level of intergenerational persistence, the two conditions are combined and the product

38 P Gregg and E Tominey, 'The wage scar of youth unemployment' (*Labour Economics*, 12 (4), 2005).

of the relationship between the components and family income and the components and earnings can be considered. The figures indicate that, with the cognitive and non-cognitive traits combined, around 30% of the persistence can be accounted for (see Figure 1), with cognitive measures making a more substantive contribution. However, the non-cognitive skills are important, especially application, self-esteem and the child's sense of personal efficacy (their sense that their own actions can make a difference rather than just fate or luck). With the introduction of educational attainment at sixteen, describing the role of school-based attainment in intergenerational persistence and the extent to which cognitive and non-cognitive factors operate through education, 40% of the persistence can be accounted for, 21% of which is coming directly through attainment at sixteen. The addition of post-compulsory education takes the total of intergenerational persistence accounted for to 46%, and the addition of labour market attachment components in the final specification takes the total accounted for to 54%.

As can be seen in Figure 1, final column, post-sixteen educational attainment is the single most important factor describing mobility, accounting for some 20%. But this is capturing a large part of the age sixteen educational attainment, as this is the gateway to post-sixteen education. Within this final specification, cognitive and non-cognitive components account for only about 6% each; the rest of their impact has come through education and labour market attachment. Labour market attachment does, in part, reflect how non-cognitive skills impact on earnings, but cognitive skills are only transmitted through education.

The level of social mobility in the UK is lower than in most other countries and decreased towards the end of the last century.

Figure 1: Decomposition of persistence; 1970 cohort

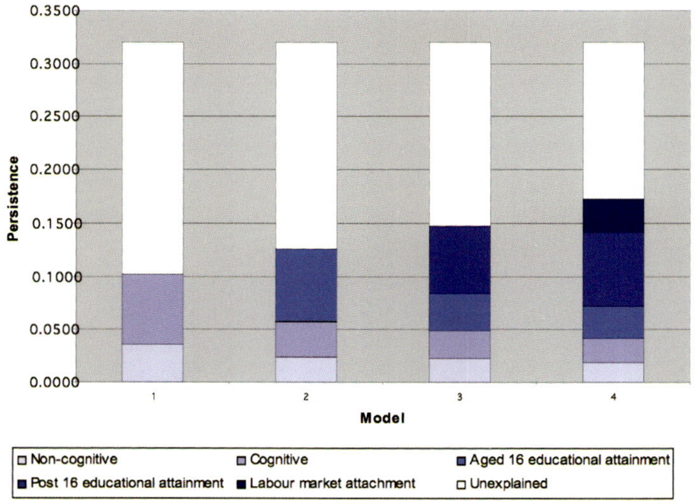

39 This is also found by F Galindo-Rueda and A Vignoles, 'The declining relative importance of ability in predicting educational attainment' (*Journal of Human Resources*, 40(2), 2005), pp. 335-353.

Legend:
- Non-cognitive
- Cognitive
- Aged 16 educational attainment
- Post 16 educational attainment
- Labour market attachment
- Unexplained

What lies behind declining mobility?

To consider this question, the second stage compares the 1958 and 1970 cohorts, using the same methodology, although, due to some data restrictions, the measurements of non-cognitive traits and educational attainment at age sixteen are slightly different to allow for comparison across time.

There are a number of noticeable differences between the two cohorts: parents' income has a weaker association with all measures of each component in the earlier of the two cohorts, and, in particular, the non-cognitive measures appear to have little or no relationship with parents' income. These components have smaller returns to earnings in both cohorts, whereas the cognitive components have larger returns to earnings in the first cohort. This suggests that inherent ability has declined in importance in determining child outcomes.[39] For the education components there has been an increase in the returns to age sixteen attainment and degree holdings, but a sharp fall in the returns to staying on post-sixteen. The impact of labour market attachment on earnings had not changed across time.

When accounting for the increase in persistence, or fall in mobility, the components considered do a good job. While persistence had increased by 0.086 points, from 0.205 to 0.291, almost 90% of the change has been accounted for (from 0.109 to 0.184). There are three main factors that account for this rise: attainment at age sixteen, through a small increase in the returns to education and a much larger increase in the relationship between family income and attainment at sixteen, accounting for 34% of the rise; access to higher education has become far more strongly related with family income and this accounts for 29%; and labour market attachment, where the scar on wages has decreased slightly but the relationship with family background has increased by a lot, accounting for 19% (see Figure 2). Non-cognitive traits are also increasingly important, again through the strengthening of the relationship with family background, but they operate mainly through educational attainment.

The components considered are successful in providing suggestive evidence of how parents with more income increasingly see their sons achieve higher earnings. It is clear that inequalities in achievements at age sixteen, in access to university and early attachment to the labour market, are increasingly important in determining the level of intergenerational mobility.

Resources need to be directed towards improving the confidence, concentration and self-efficacy of children from low-income families from an early age...

Figure 2: Decomposition of persistence across cohorts; 1958 and 1970

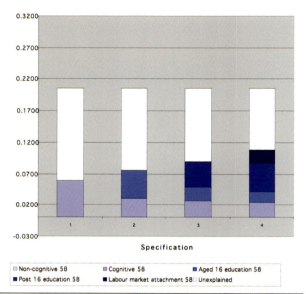

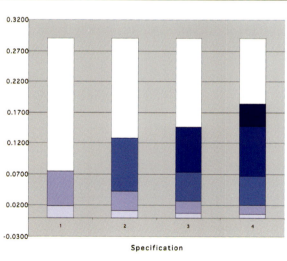

40 R J Hernstein and C
Murray, *The Bell Curve:
Intelligence and class
structure in American life* (New
York: Free Press, 1994).

41 J Heckman, J Stixrud and S
Urzua, *The effects of cognitive
and noncognitive abilities on
labor market outcomes and
social behaviour: Working
paper no. 12006* (NBER,
2006).

42 J Currie, 'Early childhood
education programs' (*Journal
of Economic Perspectives*,
15(2), 2001), pp. 213-238.

43 S Machin and S McNally,
*The Literacy Hour: Discussion
paper no. 105* (IZA, 2004).

The role of personal skills, education and early labour market attachment

The importance of the role of education in the story of intergenerational persistence somewhat overshadows the sizable role of cognitive and non-cognitive skills in accounting for this persistence. These variables both work indirectly through influencing the level of education obtained, but are nonetheless important directly as well. The strengthening of the relationship between family income and behavioural traits that inhibit children's educational attainment is one of the clear paths through which this occurs. However, cognitive ability offers no substantive contribution to changes in mobility; implying that genetically transmitted intelligence is unlikely to be a substantive driver. This evidence contrasts work by Hernstein and Murray in *The Bell Curve,*[40] which suggests that social stratification based on ability has been increasing in the twentieth century. The importance of the role of non-cognitive behaviour in later educational and labour market decisions has also been noted by Heckman, Stixrud and Urzua.[41] Their findings suggest that, in the US, schooling decisions and levels of wages given schooling decisions are strongly influenced by non-cognitive skills. They also find that 'schooling, employment, work experience and choice of occupation are affected by latent non-cognitive and cognitive skills.'

This evidence suggests that in order to raise mobility, programmes need to be developed that expand not only cognitive skills but also non-cognitive traits, such as self esteem, concentration and the child's perception of how much their lives can be influenced by their own decisions rather than chance. The strengthening of the relationship between these traits and family background suggests the need for resources to be directed towards those from deprived backgrounds.

This can be done either by directing resources exclusively at poorer schools or communities, or by universal interventions that are more effective for poor children, for example, high quality pre-school childcare[42] and the UK literacy hour.[43] High quality early years childcare and parenting are important in increasing the skills of children. The ten-year childcare strategy and Sure Start may help here, as will reducing child poverty. But more needs to be done in schools.

The government funding for education gives more resources to local education authorities (LEAs) serving poor communities, but this extra money is usually spread across all schools in the LEA rather than those teaching the most deprived children, and within school all too often extra resources are spread generally rather than targeted. The government is beginning to introduce more focused strategies. Early reading pilot schemes, the Early Reading Development Pilots, have been expanded in the pre-Budget report to include an additional 32 LEAs after initial results from the pilots suggested encouraging improvements in children's reading abilities. In addition to reading, the new pilots will also focus on speaking, listening and children's language development. Under Teach First, the best graduates are incentivised to teach in deprived schools, and this scheme is also to be expanded from the current application in London and Manchester. These small steps need to be part of a much larger direction of resources to support deprived children. The direct cash payment to schools from the Department for Education and Skills (DfES) should vary according to the extent of deprivation the school intake faces. Schools could also do more to promote home learning for disadvantaged children, as with Sure Start and Book Start.

In addition to the funding directly to schools and to programmes to help deprived areas, an emphasis needs to be placed on changing access to schooling. Currently, access to schools is largely based on a catchment area system, although there are margins of variation through faith schools, grammar schools in some areas, and other partial selection criteria. It has been shown by our research centre[44] how dramatically this creates sorting of children into schools by family income and race. Even when living near each other, the poorer child is found to go to a lower quality school than the richer child, and the poor child rarely gets into a good school, even when it is the nearest school. Fair access to good schools ought to be a key government priority. This could be achieved through greater parental choice, as long as the oversubscribed school cannot choose its preferred pupils, which suggests a lottery or clearing system as used by universities. There is also a need for an effective outreach and support for poorer families to make informed choices and enable access to good schools when they are not close by

44 S Burgess, R Harris, R Johnston and D Wilson, *Sleep-walking towards ethnic composition of English Schools, 1997-2003 – an entry cohort analysis: Working paper 06/155* (CMPO, 2006).

45 Labour Force Survey data spring 2006 (available online at: http://www.statistics. gov.uk).

46 J Blanden and S Machin, 'Educational inequality and the expansion of UK higher education' (*Scottish Journal of Political Economy*, 51(2), 2004), pp. 230-249.

(e.g. school buses).

The returns to education appear to have increased up to the mid-1990s, but recent research suggests this process has now stopped.[45] Recent Labour Force Survey data suggests that the earnings gain from getting a degree, as opposed to no qualifications, is around 50%. But the key important aspect in the story of post-sixteen education is the increase in the strength of the relationship between family income and higher education. The growing imbalance in access to higher education by family background as higher education expanded has been noted in a number of other papers. Blanden and Machin[46] use three cohorts to consider the change in the participation in higher education across time. They find, despite the fact that children from high income families were participating to the greatest extent in higher education before the expansion in the early 1990s, a disproportionate number of high income children entered higher education after the expansion, effectively widening the participation gaps between high and low income children. This supports the findings in the increase in the relationship with family background and suggests powerful evidence that this imbalance is partly driving the decline in intergenerational mobility in the UK.

Figure 3: The proportion of young people (aged 16-19) not in employment, full-time education or training across time

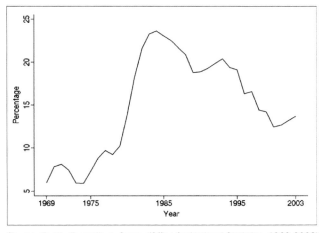

Source: *Family Expenditure Survey* (Office for National Statistics, 1969-2003).

Policy interventions that could, therefore, enable those from low income families to stay on at school and achieve higher education could lead to an increase in mobility. The number of sixteen to nineteen year olds in the UK who are classified as NEETs (not in employment, education or training) rose sharply through the early 1980s recession, peaking in 1985, with a smaller peak after the early 1990s in 1993, and then fell sharply with rising employment and education participation (see Figure 3). Since 1997, according to the Labour Force Survey (LFS), the proportion of sixteen to nineteen year olds NEETs has increased slightly, from 11.5% to 12.1% by 2006. As can be seen from Figure 4, those from the lowest social classes are far more likely to fall into this category than those from the highest social classes.

There is still a strong relationship between family background, education and early labour market attachment. A report by the DfES found that the pilot schemes of educational maintenance allowances (EMAs) had little effect on drawing back young people who entered the NEET group at the end of compulsory school education, and those in receipt of EMA tended to be better qualified on entry to college. Therefore EMA may encourage poorer children with qualifications to stay on in education, but it is not tackling the problem of those who are disengaged from an early age. Evidence from the LFS suggests that, of those who were NEETs in 2006, 30% had achieved no qualifications and 37% had left school after their GCSEs. The bulk of NEETs, some 58%, are currently unemployed (though many are not on job seeker's allowance, as many will be ineligible), suggesting around 8% of the overall age group are unemployed. Of the remaining NEETs, 11% were sick or disabled and 13% were looking after the home, mostly with children.

47 Op.cit., ref. 38.

Figure 4: Decomposition of activities young people (aged 16-19) are participating in, by social class of the head of the family for 2006

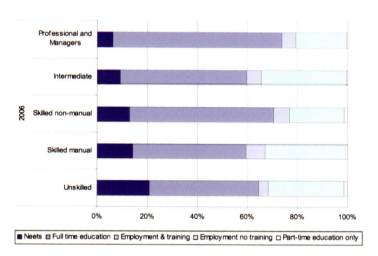

Source: *Labour Force Survey* (Office for National Statistics, 2006).

Gregg and Tominey[47] found that unemployment in youth in the early 1980s caused a wage scar on individuals, even at the age of 42, of between 12% and 15%. If the individuals avoid repeated occurrences of unemployment, the wage scar is still around 8-10%. Their research suggests that this wage scar was caused directly by their unemployment rather than by unobserved characteristics of these individuals. Hence NEETs can expect to have near-lifelong wage and employment scars. Young men's early labour market attachment across the two birth cohorts (1958 and 1970) saw a strong increase in the relationship with family background. This means that there has been an increasing concentration of those experiencing unemployment among low income families, and is hence associated with reduced intergenerational mobility.

The stubborn resistance of the numbers of youths not in education or employment requires addressing. There are two approaches that could be taken, which need not be alternatives. First, since the last Conservative government ended the entitlement of sixteen and seventeen year olds to unemployment benefits, there has been no contact mechanism with these individuals if they choose to leave education. The Labour government created EMAs, payments for young people from poor families who stay on in education, and tax credits, likewise, are available for those in education. However, this has mainly resulted in a switch to education from young people who would alternatively have entered into employment (usually without training), rather than reducing the group of NEETs. One problem is making contact with the NEETs to bring them back in to work or education; those who leave the system at sixteen can be unheard of for two years and contact is only re-established if they claim unemployment benefit when they reach eighteen. Unlike the welfare-to-work programmes for other groups, there is no benefit link to incentivise contact and participation. So an effective policy would be to create an activity-related benefit for sixteen to seventeen year olds whereby young people receive a payment when meeting the conditions of studying (already available under EMA), training or undertaking a preparatory stage. This last element would cover waiting for a programme to start, basic skills training, work trials etc., and would be an individualised support package designed by a personalised adviser. Payments would be conditional on fulfilling the agreement. This voluntary approach would also reduce the bias towards full-time education over employment with training that exists for EMAs. The other alternative is a compulsory approach, raising the school leaving age to eighteen but including workplace employment with training (e.g. the Train to Gain programme) within the system of fourteen to nineteen education. This proposal would also make a contribution to equalising children's life chances.

The expansion of university education has benefited children from the most affluent 50% of families, with very little impact on the poorest. But the bulk of this gap in participation stems from earlier educational disadvantage that builds through children's school years. This increasing attainment gap is not due to a widening gap in innate ability but, rather, increasing differences in family resources, part of which are used to get children into the best schools.

The most effective way to improve intergenerational mobility is to expand educational opportunities of the deprived, which, as well as its direct effects, will also raise the supply of skills and, in turn, reduce the wage mark-up for education qualifications (reducing wage inequalities, and hence differences in life chances). Measures to improve participation beyond age sixteen are also important to aiding this process. Current plans to offer help with funding at HE level to those who complete a 40-week voluntary service, and new 'earn to learn' packages that offer support to those who study for HE qualifications part-time and work part-time, could prove beneficial in increasing the number of participants in HE from low-income families. In addition, the fact that there is now a grant offered to those from low-income families who attend HE institutions is a step in the right direction, but the low level of this grant and the complexity of bursary systems run by each university separately need to be addressed to open the system to those from poorer backgrounds.

Conclusion

To conclude, the level of social mobility in the UK is lower than in most other countries and decreased towards the end of the last century. In order to address this trend, it is important to understand the components that account for this reduction in life chances. The evidence suggests that there are three key components influencing this downturn in mobility: educational attainment at sixteen; access to higher education; and early labour market experiences. Underlying these three components is the role played by personal skills in early to mid-childhood, which, through non-cognitive traits (application, self-esteem and a sense of personal efficacy) becoming more strongly related to family background, are playing a more important role in pre-dicting life chances in the later cohort.

With this in mind, there are a number of areas where policy needs to become more focused. To tackle the issue of the increasing relationship between family background and non-cognitive traits, resources need to be directed towards improving the confidence, concentration and self-efficacy of children from low-income families from an early age through higher quality childcare and pre-school programmes. Tackling child poverty may well have major benefits in this area. Better funding for deprived schools, fairer access policies to schools, and increased funding to schemes like 'teach first' would allow poorer children greater access to better quality education and better quality teachers. This would improve the educational attainment of low-income children and increase mobility in two ways: by reducing the relationship between attainment and family background; and by widening the supply of more qualified individuals, and hence diminishing the returns to education witnessed at present. In addition, as the number of NEETs continues to be a problem, increasing the compulsory school leaving age to eighteen and/or introducing an activity-related benefit for sixteen and seventeen year olds would create a contact mechanism with those who are currently out of reach to reduce the impact of wage scarring on them in later life. Policies aimed at encouraging participation from low-income children in HE, such as fee reductions for voluntary work and more flexible part-time options, will also increase mobility by increasing access to higher education, therefore reducing the returns to education and the relationship between family background and further attainment.

5. Harnessing the aspirations of sick and disabled people: the story so far and a look into the future

Dr Roy Sainsbury

48 Department of Social Security, *New Ambitions for Our Country: A new contract for welfare* (TSO, 1998).

Introduction

The title of this collection is *The Politics of Aspiration.* It is a title that immediately attracted me when I was invited to contribute an essay based on many years' experience of research on welfare-to-work programmes aimed at helping sick and disabled people enter employment. The attraction was that word *aspiration,* because from the work that I and many colleagues have done it has consistently emerged as central to helping people into work. I do not think it is too much of a simplification to say that without aspiration to move towards work, progress is highly unlikely. The positive thing about aspiration is that it can be harnessed if it is there from the start, but it can also be instilled and nurtured if it isn't. The other side of the coin, though, is that aspiration can be a delicate thing, easily damaged or, worse, destroyed.

So, in this essay I want to look at what happens to people out of work because of a health or disabling condition when their aspirations (or lack of) come into contact with government social security and employment policies. In doing so I will be starting an unfinished story that started in 1997 with the New Labour government's Green Paper, *New Ambitions for Our Country: A new contract for welfare,*[48] reaching its latest instalment in 2006 with *A New Deal for Welfare: Empowering people to work,*[49] a document that has formed the basis of the 2006 Welfare Reform Bill, which is due to become law in 2007.

I will start with an overview of welfare-to-work policies for sick and disabled people since 1997. This will identify one major piece of unfinished business – reform of incapacity benefit – that is part of the Welfare Reform Bill mentioned above. The third section therefore looks at the replacement for incapacity benefit, the employment and support allowance, that links to section four, which offers a long-term vision of how this might lead to more radical benefit reform.

Welfare to work, sickness and disability

One of the most pressing social policy issues facing the Labour government in 1997 was the seemingly unstoppable rise in the number of people receiving long-term incapacity benefit. The reasons for this rise were reasonably well understood. Large numbers of new claimants were generated by the closure of mines and heavy industry in the 1980s and 1990s, claimants were encouraged to claim sickness-related benefits rather than unemployment benefits, and, importantly, far more claimants were coming on to benefits than were leaving, creating a large 'stock' of long-term recipients with no recent experience of the labour market.

The government's response was to create the New Deal for Disabled People (NDDP) in 1998. The core idea of NDDP was to offer to people in receipt of incapacity benefit for six months or more individual, customised help, from a designated 'personal adviser' whose job it was to ascertain a person's aspirations, assess their capabilities, identify barriers to work and put into action a plan intended to get that person a sustainable paid job. This model of delivery based on a personal adviser borrowed heavily from the New Deals for young people and for lone parents. The personal advisers were intended to be entrepreneurial in their approach. They could mobilise existing resources already available through Jobcentre Plus, and had a pot of money that they could use creatively at their discretion to address any particular needs (for example, for clothing, tools or fares).

Unfortunately, although many individuals benefited greatly

49 Department for Work and Pensions, *A New Deal for Welfare: Empowering people to work* (TSO, 2006).

50 Department for Work
and Pensions, *Pathways to
Work: Helping people into
employment* (TSO, 2002).

from involvement with NDDP, the numbers of people taking
it up were disappointing. Part of the problem was thought to
reside in the scheme's voluntary nature. The NDDP provider
organisations could only publicise their services and wait for
responses. Not enough people did, and new policy thinking was
required.

The next big step forward came in 2002 with the publica-
tion of the policy document *Pathways to Work: Helping people into
employment*.[50] At the outset, the thinking behind *Pathways* attracted (cautious) support from a wide range of sources, including
the disability lobby. One of the good things about the Pathways
approach was that it seemed to reflect lessons learned over the
previous five years. The architecture of the Pathways to Work
scheme reflected most (not quite all) of these lessons. In its initial manifestation (it has evolved since) Pathways contained the
following elements:

- a new breed of personal adviser, selected and specially trained
  to be able to work with incapacity benefit recipients expected to
  present a wide range of health and other barriers to work
- a focus on new claimants of incapacity benefit, not those who
  had been in receipt for long periods
- a new service – the condition management programme –
  designed to provide support and advice, through partnership with
  the NHS, to help people understand their conditions and their
  capabilities better
- a new financial incentive – the return to work credit – of £40 a
  week for a year for people commencing work of sixteen hours a
  week or more
- access to the full range of services already available through
  Jobcentre Plus, including NDDP, Access to Work, training opportunities (and much more)
- a regime of six *compulsory* work-focused interviews with a
  personal adviser.

Pathways to Work started out as a pilot scheme in seven areas of
the country in 2004, but decisions were soon taken to make it
bigger, based on early administrative information that showed
that incapacity benefit claimants in the pilot areas were coming
off benefit at a rate some eight percentage points more than
non-pilot areas. Ministers were delighted. Nothing tried previ-

ously could match this order of impact. At the time of writing, Pathways has been expanded to fourteen further areas and to some longer-term recipients (those on benefit for between one and three years), and the scheme will begin to go nationwide in 2007. Furthermore, confirmation of the early administrative data has been provided from a survey of incapacity benefit claimants carried out as part of the Pathways evaluation. The Pathways policy increased the percentage of people working (at around ten months after first contacting a local Jobcentre Plus office) by an estimated nine percentage points.[51]

So, why is Pathways having the level of impact it is so far? The answers to this question are beginning to emerge from the large programme of evaluation research that has been going on since Pathways began. For the purposes of this essay, I will concentrate very briefly on two related topics – the personal adviser-claimant relationship, and the compulsory regime of work-focused interviews. I have selected these because they are relevant to the theme of aspiration and to government plans to reform incapacity benefit.

When incapacity benefit personal advisers were interviewed as part of the evaluation research they were able to discuss a number of factors that were influential in moving people forwards towards work. The research report[52] highlighted the importance the advisers put in the personal relationship between themselves and their clients and the need to establish a 'positive trusting relationship' that might only come after a number of interviews with them. One adviser was quoted as saying: 'You've got to get the trust from them and then they'll open up to you and discuss any issues they've got with you… You've got to do it over a period of time.'[53]

This view of the importance of the adviser-client relationship is echoed in research with Pathways clients.[54] Among some social security recipients there is a widespread distrust of the Department for Work and Pensions and Jobcentre Plus. Many people view the benefit authorities suspiciously, more concerned to reduce or stop benefit than to help them. People on incapacity benefit, in particular, fear that a willingness on their part to discuss a possible return to work will be taken as evidence that they no longer qualify for incapacity benefit. People generally need to be convinced that personal advisers are 'on their side'

51 S Adam, C Emmerson, C Frayne and A Goodman, *Early Quantitative Evidence on the Impact of the Pathways to Work Pilot, Research report 354* (DWP, 2006).

52 T Knight, S Dickens, M Mitchell, and K Woodfield, *Incapacity Benefit Reforms – the personal adviser role and practices: Stage two, Research report 278* (DWP, 2005).

53 Ibid., p.19

54 A Corden and K Nice, *Pathways to Work: Findings from the final cohort in a qualitative longitudinal panel of incapacity benefits recipients, Research Report 398* (DWP, 2006).

55 Op cit., ref. 52.

and not there to police their benefit. This relationship of trust is sometimes hard won, and personal advisers are reluctant to jeopardise it. One feature of Pathways that helps foster trust is the voluntary nature of any involvement with anything other than the work-focused interviews. No one is obliged to take up any of the opportunities, such as the condition management programme or NDDP, if they do not want to.

The role of the personal adviser is, therefore, what has been described as an 'enabler'.[55] Personal advisers do have a contrasting 'enforcer' role in connection with the work-focused interviews. As mentioned above, attendance at these is compulsory and failure to attend can lead to benefit being suspended. This compulsion to attend interviews was a cause of concern to some disability organisations when Pathways began, but in practice has proved largely unproblematic for personal advisers and clients alike. Hence, personal advisers have been able to balance their enabler/enforcer roles in a way that also allows a trusting relationship to develop. One might call the level of compulsion within Pathways to Work as 'light touch'. There is only compulsion to talk to a personal adviser, which for most people is neither a problem nor an imposition.

What has emerged from the research with personal advisers and Pathways clients is that, as minister after minister has repeated, many people on incapacity benefits have aspirations to return to work. The strength of Pathways so far appears to be that, in practice, it is working with the grain of people's aspirations, helping them identify work goals and enabling them to achieve those goals at a pace that they determine, rather than is forced upon them.

Having said that, the barriers to work posed by the benefit system, identified before Pathways but not addressed by the Pathways scheme, have remained. Remained, that is, until the announcements of the government's plan to replace incapacity benefit with a new benefit. The next part of the essay turns its focus, therefore, on to the imminent arrival of the employment and support allowance.

Reforming incapacity benefit

The reform of incapacity benefit, currently part of the Welfare Reform Bill, is probably well overdue. In an article written for the *Disability Rights Bulletin* in 2006, I summarised what I saw as the problems with the benefit.

As a means for providing a secure and adequate income for people who cannot work the current hotch-potch of piecemeal and overlapping benefits doesn't actually perform very well. And as an active rather than passive system, supporting people who want to move towards and into work, it struggles to perform at all.[56]

This is by no means a maverick thought. In introducing its plans for reform in the green paper, *A New Deal For Welfare*,[57] the government listed 'fundamental problems' with incapacity benefit. One of these was the 'perverse incentive' for people to stay on incapacity benefit rather than seek a route off it and into work. This perverse incentive works in a number of ways, for example, by paying more money to longer-term recipients, and by introducing the possibility of people losing their benefit if they even try to return to work.

There are other problems with the benefit also. The medical test (called the personal capability assessment, or PCA) is perceived to be arbitrary and difficult to administer. It is badly suited to people with mental health conditions or fluctuating conditions. As a result of 'passing' or 'failing' the PCA people are obliged to move back and forth between incapacity benefit and job seeker's allowance. One consequence of this is that someone receiving some form of help on the basis of being an incapacity benefit recipient can have that help removed. People are afraid to try work on a temporary or trial basis because they fear they will lose their incapacity benefit.

The proposed replacement for incapacity benefit is called the employment and support allowance. It is planned to be implemented in 2008. In essence the ESA is structured into three elements. New claimants will be paid a 'holding rate' (at the same level as JSA) until they have been assessed under a revised personal capability assessment. The new PCA will distinguish between those claimants who will receive a higher rate payment and *not* be required to satisfy any work-related requirements as a condition of receipt, and those who have less serious health or disabling conditions who *will* be required to draw up an action plan of work-related activities, for which they will be

56 R Sainsbury, 'Long-term benefits reform – should a single working age benefit be the aim?' (*Disability Rights Bulletin*, Spring 2006), pp.3-5.

57 Op.cit., ref. 49.

58 Ibid., p. 92.

paid a lower rate. Sanctions will be applicable to claimants failing to comply with their action plan.

Unsurprisingly, the proposals for ESA attracted some criticism and concern. From a personal perspective, when I read the green paper in January 2006 I was also puzzled at the proposals for ESA because they did not seem to address the problems with incapacity benefit that the government had itself identified and had also emerged from research on incapacity benefit and Pathways to Work over a number of years. How, I thought, would ESA solve the problem of people with fluctuating conditions and the problem of moving between JSA and the new benefit? And wouldn't a 'perverse incentive' still operate because a higher rate of benefit would be paid to the most sick and disabled claimants? And wouldn't people still be worried that any attempts to move towards work would result in a loss of benefit?

In some ways, therefore, the ESA proposals seemed like a missed opportunity for more radical reform that would transform incapacity benefit into a much more active benefit that supported welfare-to-work policies rather than perpetuated the constraining features of incapacity benefit. However, a very short chapter in the green paper seemed to suggest that ESA was not the end of the story but that longer-term reform was very much part of the government's thinking.

So having reached the end of the story so far, the next section takes a tentative look into the future at what that longer-term reform could produce.

A look into the future – a single 'working age benefit'?

The one sentence in the green paper that grabbed my attention was this:

We consider that there may be advantages in moving in the longer term towards a single system of benefits for all people of working age, with appropriate additions for those who have caring responsibilities and those with a long-term illness or disability.[58]

Questions were immediately prompted. Could a single 'working age benefit' be designed that would be appropriate for all working age claimants, whether they are simply unemployed or lone parents or disabled people? What might it look like? Could it fit with welfare-to-work policies and support people's moves into work rather than hinder them? Elsewhere[59] I have attempted to answer these questions, but in the space available here I will summarise the main points. First, I suggest that a 'working age benefit' could be based on three principles:

- a single set of rules
- benefit paid at a standard basic rate (with additions based on defined circumstances)
- benefit remains the same over time (i.e. no higher, long-term rates).

59 Op.cit., ref. 56, pp.3-5.

Such a benefit would be easier to understand and to administer than either incapacity benefit or ESA. The problems created by moving between job seeker's allowance and incapacity benefit would disappear and there would be no risk to benefit of trying work, as the benefit would be the same before and after a period in work. The stigma, and resultant discrimination, sometimes associated with the name 'incapacity benefit' might be avoided. And there would be no 'incentives' for claiming one benefit over another. The next question to address was the level of conditionality that should be attached to a 'working age benefit' – what should the *responsibilities* of claimants be?

Supposing eligibility was based on the answers a claimant gave to what I have called two 'gateway questions':

- Do you think you will be capable of paid work at any time in the future?
- Do you want to work at any time in the future?

The evidence suggests that most people would answer yes to both. This could be the basis of a Jobcentre Plus personal adviser and a claimant working together to achieve the same thing, work in the future, concentrating on the adviser's 'enabler' role. Threats about sanctions would be irrelevant. The adviser-claimant relationship would be based on the aspirations of the individual, not on a preconception of what he or she ought to do. This approach is potentially highly inclusive and non-discriminatory. No one need be labelled as 'a lone parent' or 'disabled person' or anything else. Clearly some criteria would need to be established whereby a 'no' to either question would not necessarily exclude a person from receiving the working age benefit. There are circumstances relating to health or disability for which a no to the first question would be entirely legitimate. The current incapacity benefit PCA and proposed revised PCA under the ESA perform a similar function to what would be needed for a working age benefit. The attraction of the 'gateway' questions is that they reflect most people's aspirations to work rather than being based on a presumption that conditions and sanctions are necessary to move people towards work.

These ideas are, appropriately for this volume, at the level of aspiration rather than detail. To turn aspiration into practical policy would require a number of tricky issues to be addressed, such as the level of benefits, whether eligibility should be linked to national insurance contributions or means tested, and what additions (for example for disability or caring responsibilities, or to reflect the additional costs of disability) should be available. The question to be answered at this stage is whether the potential advantages of a working age benefit over both incapacity benefit and ESA justifies time and effort to address the tricky issues.

Conclusion

This has been an opportune time to look at welfare reform and disabled people. The government is currently taking stock after nearly ten years of quite intensive policy change, which not only includes the types of welfare-to-work policies I have been discussing in this essay but also the introduction of the minimum wage, tax credits, and the implementation and development of the Disability Discrimination Act. The major changes in welfare-to-work and disability benefits have been mirrored in pensions policy, child support and housing benefit. This is not to suggest that the government is complacent about what it has achieved to date. It has set itself ambitious targets for the eradication of child poverty by 2020, an overall employment rate of 80% of the population, and the reduction in the number of people on incapacity benefits by one million, all of which look highly daunting as I write in late 2006.

Looking across the brief of the Department for Work and Pensions, therefore, it is clear why it is taking stock now and why the Secretary of State, John Hutton, announced on 18

December 2006 'a long-term review of the government's welfare to work strategy to tackle economic inactivity and promote social mobility'.[60] It is a pity, therefore, that long-term benefit reform (subsequent to the introduction of ESA in 2008) has seemingly already been judged a non-starter. Referring to the same sentence from the green paper that I have cited above and which encouraged my long-term thinking, the Secretary of State told the Select Committee on Work and Pensions on 6 March 2006:

We are not talking about there simply being one working-age benefit. Some people have looked at this part of the Green Paper and have assumed that there will only be one working age benefit; that is not what I think is likely to come out of this… The Employment and Support Allowance is a long-term reform of Incapacity Benefit and provides a much more straightforward, streamlined, simpler form of supporting people on Incapacity Benefit.[61]

Not many commentators have endorsed this view of ESA as 'more straightforward, streamlined [and] simpler', so it is hopefully not too late to persuade policymakers that long-term benefit reform is not only achievable but actually necessary to support the aims of helping more people on incapacity benefits into work. As I have documented above, the Pathways to Work approach has produced not only an increase in people coming off incapacity benefit and into work, but also a depth of understanding about how Pathways gets results. Building a trusting, mutually co-operative relationship that allows aspirations to be nurtured and realised is an essential element when Pathways works well. Much has been achieved, but as always, there is still more to be done. Space has prevented me tackling the role of employers and the impact of labour markets on the employment prospects of incapacity benefit recipients, and these are clearly highly important issues.

Jim Murphy, Minister for Employment and Welfare Reform, speaking in the Committee stage of the Welfare Reform Bill in October 2006, referred to the 'overwhelming aspiration of those on incapacity benefit' of whom 'nine out of ten… say that they wish for the opportunity to work.' Harnessing that aspiration should ideally be at the heart of not

60 DWP, 'Hutton launches wide-ranging welfare review' (available online at: www.dwp.gov.uk/mediacentre/pressreleases/2006/dec/wel01-181206.asp).

61 Select Committee on Work and Pensions, *Incapacity Benefits and Pathways to Work: Third report* (TSO, 2006).

only employment policies like Pathways to Work, but also social security policy. It would be a highly retrograde step if imminent incapacity benefit reform should stifle aspiration by jeopardising the relationship between advisers and claimants when there is the opportunity of strengthening it by creative long-term thinking about further benefit reform.

6. Cultures, belief and aspiration

Trevor Phillips

The new government in 1997 opened up the prospect of a change for Britain – a new focus on the betterment of society's disadvantaged. This government has aimed to secure a standard of living for all citizens commensurate with the dignity and worth of each human being. It is increasingly evident, however, that aspects of identity distinct from social class have had, and continue to have, significant implications for people's life chances and their risk of experiencing poverty. It is also apparent that this matters more and more.

A number of the policies introduced since 1997 have made an important contribution to realising the Labour government's early ambitions. The UK now has the fourth highest employment rate in the EU. The national minimum wage, introduced in 1999, has boosted the pay of low-paid workers. The New Deal programmes have provided a mix of employment incentives to particular client groups and employers. While it is impossible to attribute the increased labour market participation of particular groups solely to the New Deal,[62] since 1997 employment rates have gone up across all those groups that were targeted by these programmes.[63] More than 500 Sure Start programmes are up and running in some of the most deprived areas of the country, designed to improve the life chances of children by improving their health and social development and ensuring that they are ready to learn when they get to school.

This government can point to many important accomplishments and, since 1997, has reduced the numbers of people liv-

62 J Hills, K Stewart, (eds.), *A More Equal Society? New Labour, poverty, inequality and exclusion* (Policy Press, 2005).

63 Department for Work and Pensions, *Opportunity for All: Seventh annual report* (TSO, 2005).

64 M Brewer, A Goodman, J Shaw and L Sibieta, *Poverty and Inequality in Britain* (Institute for Fiscal Studies, 2006).

65 J Hills, *Inequality and the State* (Oxford University Press, 2004).

66 J Blanden, P Gregg and S Machin, 'Educational inequality and intergenerational mobility' in S Machin and A Vignoles, *What's the Good of Education? The economics of education in the UK* (Princeton University Press, 2005).

67 J Goldthorpe and C Mills, 'Trends in intergenerational class mobility in Britain in the late twentieth century' in R Breen, (ed.), *Social Mobility in Europe* (Oxford University Press, 2004).

ing in poverty. However, it is also faced with the stark fact that the gap between the richest and the poorest in Britain has failed to narrow over the past decade. The truth is that change is slow and hard. According to the Institute of Fiscal Studies, income inequality rose to perhaps its highest ever levels in the first five years of the Labour administration before falling back to the same levels seen in 1996-97.[64]

Broadly speaking, over the past 60 years, life for most Britons has improved. On average, we live longer, we are healthier, we are better educated and many people enjoy a lifestyle never available to their parents. Moreover, today we are far less likely to be trapped by the accident of our birth, which at the start of the last century would have made our careers, incomes and social status largely dependent on those of our parents. Wider social and economic change has opened opportunities for many less well-off families. Increased access to educational opportunities and programmes to give children a better start in life mean that, though socioeconomic status is still probably the best predictor of our fortunes, it no longer imposes the ironclad certainty of failure or success that it once did.

Of men born in the 1950s, only 13% moved to a lower social class than their parents while 42% experienced upward mobility (36% for women born in the 1950s).[65] However, examinations of absolute social mobility comparing more recent cohorts suggest that this historic shift has run out of steam in recent years. Analysis from the national child development study (which focused on children born in a specific week in 1958) and from the birth cohort study (which did the same for children born in one week in 1970) demonstrates that children born to poorer families in 1970 were more likely to remain relatively poorer as adults than children born from poorer families in 1958.[66] The most authoritative studies have concluded that: 'it is difficult to see evidence of a continuing increase in the total mobility rate post-1972'.[67]

Alongside this, many Britons still do not achieve even the social and economic minima in income, education, health and housing. Large numbers do not have access to essential entitlements, and all too frequently institutions fall short of basic human rights standards. Several areas of disadvantage have proved especially obstinate, and have not so far responded to policy. For example, people with the lowest levels of qualifications as a group have consistently, over the past few years, experienced rising levels of unemployment against a trend of increasing employment for other groups.

As well as these limitations on our progress, other powerful drivers for social and economic inequality have emerged. As Chair of the forthcoming Commission for Equality and Human Rights, I am principally concerned with the fact that levels of material comfort are unevenly distributed, not only by socio-economic group, but also by factors like age, disability, gender and race. In some cases these factors may be the cause of disadvantage by themselves, without any contribution from socio-economic status.

Three areas of failure stand out: politics, business and the media. In Parliament, for example, there are fifteen ethnic minority MPs (2.3% compared to 7.9% in the general population), in business there are 121 directorships held by women in FTSE 100 companies (10.5%) and only four are held by women from an ethnic minority background, and in the media only 13% of editors of national newspapers are female.[68] This is hardly surprising, given that this trinity probably represents the nexus of power in most western societies. Exclusion from the decision-making levels of these fields is the clearest indication possible of an imbalance of power within our society.

Over the past 40 years we have introduced new measures, including anti-discrimination law, to tackle some non-socioeconomic markers of disadvantage – ethnicity and race, gender, disability, sexual orientation and, latterly, age, religion and belief. Legal measures have had some positive effects. But law by itself has had limited success in dislodging some of the most stubborn penalties.

Though anti-discrimination laws and other measures have reduced some gaps, others have not closed, and others have opened up. For example, the employment penalties faced by women as a group have steadily reduced over time. But other penalties have increased over the past 30 years – penalties associated with ethnicity, disability and age were higher in the 1990s than in the 1970s.[69] Most alarming is that in some groups (most frequently, but not exclusively, defined by race or religion) disadvantage is effectively being passed from parent to child.

68 Equal Opportunities Commission, *Sex and Power: Who runs Britain?* (EOC, 2006).

69 R Berthoud and M Blekesaune, *Persistent Employment Disadvantage, 1974-2003* (ISER Working Paper, University of Essex, March 2006).

70 *Interim report for consultation* (The Equalities Review, March 2006).

71 Labour Force Survey, *Quarterly Supplement,* Autumn 2005 (available online at: http://www.statistics.gov.uk/statbase/Expodata/Spreadsheets/D7910.xls).

72 However, analysis of unemployment rates (the number of women looking for work) shows Caribbean women disadvantaged with respect to white women.

Clear patterns of inequalities in employment over time can be seen from an analysis reviewing data over a 30-year period.[70] The analysis was targeted at the disadvantage, or 'penalty', associated with disability, ethnicity or gender, correcting for other characteristics.

Taking as the 'base case' the normally most favoured group – non-disabled partnered white men below the age of 50 – in almost all circumstances this group outperforms every other (including single men) when it comes to labour market participation. Broadly speaking, over the 30-year period, almost all the chosen characteristics showed some employment gaps, and both the employment gaps and the penalties associated with age and ethnicity have become larger over the past 30 years.

Overall, there is an employment gap between ethnic minority people of working age and Whites of around 17%, with Whites standing at about 76% and ethnic minorities at around 59%.[71] However, the picture is not as simple as this would suggest – there is considerable variation among ethnic groups and by gender.

Detailed analysis throws up some important findings. Surprisingly, if we compare the employment rates of Caribbean people with those of Whites there is, consistently, little overall difference – to all intents and purposes there is no net employment penalty for Caribbean people. Indeed, in the early 1980s Caribbeans were more likely to be employed than Whites. This unexpected finding is partly accounted for by the fact that most previous analyses concentrated on male employment. Analysis of employment penalties for Caribbean people by gender shows that Caribbean men are now indeed consistently less likely to be employed than Whites. This is a real penalty of around 4-5%, accounted for entirely by ethnicity. Conversely, Caribbean women are more likely to be employed than comparable White women; that is to say, White women show an employment penalty relative to Caribbean women.[72] However, in other cases the impact of ethnicity is much more significant.

There are three groups who the analysis shows are especially vulnerable in relation to labour market exclusion. The first are people of Pakistani and Bangladeshi heritage. Pakistani and Bangladeshi men suffered no serious employment penalty compared to Whites in the 1970s, but by the mid-1990s their employment penalty had risen to 13%, though it has lessened slightly in recent years. Pakistani and Bangladeshi women suffer a much greater penalty compared to their White counterparts. Even after discounting the fact that they are more likely to have young children, their employment penalty during the past 30 years ranges between 24% and 35% (though there is a small recent decrease, falling from 35% in 1996 to 31% in 2001).

The second group shown by this research to be especially disadvantaged are disabled people. The measure of disability used in the General Household Survey is a broad one, and it is plausible that disabled people with more significant impairments are more disadvantaged. The proportion of disabled people with a job declined from just over 60% in 1974, to only 45% in 1995. And employment rates among non-disabled people have risen during the period, increasing the gap from 12% to 33% in 2003. Though some of this gap can be explained by factors not directly related to disability, such as age and qualifications, the employment penalty associated purely with disability leapt from just 5% to about 18% in the mid-990s. It has steadied since then, but has not declined significantly.

However, the employment penalties associated with disability and ethnicity look positively benign when set against those faced by women with children. Over the last 30 years, the employment penalties faced by women as a group have steadily reduced over time. This trend was not caused by changes in the employment prospects for single women without children, or women with a partner but no children, whose penalties relative to partnered men remained more or less steady. It is the change in the labour market presence of the most disadvantaged women - mothers, especially of young children – that accounts for the bulk of the change for women overall. The penalty faced by mothers of young children with a partner fell from 69% in 1975 relative to partnered men to 40% in 2002 – a huge fall, but from a very high base. It is worth stressing that men's employment rates are unaffected by fatherhood. Simply put, for women, the birth of a child is a major trigger episode that produces a long-lasting penalty; for men it is not.

Comparing labour market participation of older and younger workers, we can see that in the mid-1970s older workers experienced a penalty of about 3.5%; by 1995 this had

73 National Statistics,
Family Resources Survey
(Department for Work and
Pensions, 2005).

74 Tom Sefton, 'Give and
take: Public attitudes to
redistribution' in Alison Park,
(ed.), *22nd Report of the
British Social Attitudes Survey*
(Sage, 2005).

75 *A New Pension Settlement
for the Twenty-first Century*
(Pensions Commission,
2005).

76 *Excluded Older People:
Social Exclusion Unit Interim
Report* (Social Exclusion Unit,
2005).

grown to 8.5%, where it has remained more or less constant since then. For older people, there is a clear link between earlier life events and opportunities and outcomes in older age; for example, the link between income in retirement and absences from the labour market during working age, or the impact of education and socioeconomic status on resilience in older age. For people over 60, the group with the greatest net and physical wealth are those aged 60 to 64 – the group with the least are those aged 80 and over.[73] Over the last eight years pensioners' incomes have risen faster than earnings.[74] However, on current trends, by 2035 only one-third of older people will have sufficient incomes to avoid the need for support from means-tested benefits.[75] Lower lifetime earnings for women mean lower contributions and lower pensions. Older people from ethnic minorities, particularly those from Bangladeshi and Pakistani communities, are three times more likely to have below-average income and are twice as likely to be in the lowest income quintile in old age.[76]

Beyond the personal or individual impact of these inequalities on large swathes of Britain's population, what does this all mean for us as a nation? The economic and demographic context puts into stark perspective just how important these issues are for everybody's continued wellbeing. Increasingly, this context has a global dimension; it involves change at a structural level; it is moved and shaped by forces that are integral to the development of a modern post-industrial nation in an age of globalisation.

The labour market has changed radically in recent decades. A reduction in the number of manufacturing vacancies and a rise in service sector jobs have made more job opportunities available to women. However, the very nature of those jobs has given rise to new inequalities – with more women in part-time, low-paid work. The move towards a higher added-value, knowledge-based economy in the UK, coupled with the educational underperformance by boys, disabled people and by some ethnic minority communities, could signal the emergence of significant new kinds of inequality based on gender, disability and race. Failure to capture the potential contribution of all these groups of individuals could, in itself, emerge as a significant obstacle to growth and competitiveness over the medium and long term. It is estimated that, by 2010, only a fifth of the workforce will be what is currently considered the 'default' employee – that is white, non-disabled, male and under 45.[77]

So, whether the question is observed by a progressive concerned with fairness and social justice, or from a dispassionate Benthamite stance concerned only with our economic development, it is evident that equality matters more and more for Britain. The case should be increasingly self-evident, and our collective failure to turn warm words into concrete action is increasingly untenable. By action, I do not mean that we should continue tinkering at the edges creating concessions that allow more of us to operate like the 'default' employee. Too often, measures to improve equality in the workplace equate to making it easier for women, for example, to better fit into a pattern of working that was set by and for men. But given the demographic changes that will transform the face of our workplaces over the next few years, it is not feasible for yesterday's default employee to set the rules. For this reason, it is no longer enough to make better umbrellas for the disadvantaged; instead we must change the weather. If not, we risk falling behind as a nation unable to sustain ongoing economic development. This is not a minority concern; it truly matters for everybody.

Law, leadership and gradual cultural change have gone some way in tackling discrimination per se – although progress has been uneven across the different dimensions of inequality and in different aspects of life, economic and otherwise. The more recent equality legislation has sought to go further than merely preventing discrimination towards actively remedying deficits and promoting equality. This theme of proactivity, starting with the race equality duty placed on public authorities by the Race Relations Act (2000), has now started to dominate discourse on race equality. It is increasingly well understood that, while remedies for discrimination against individuals are crucial, they have failed to make a dent in the aggregate disadvantages suffered by various groups. We must address the structural factors that give rise to persistent disadvantage.

One way in which a proactive stance could be put into practice would be through greater use of the – relatively neglected – positive action measures that were allowed for in

77 Office of National Statistics, *British Labour Market Projections* (ONS, 1998).

78 *Interim Report for Consultation* (The Equalities Review, March 2006).

the 1976 Race Relations Act. This provision permits employers to encourage applications from a particular racial group, or offer training, if that group has been severely underrepresented in a certain type of work over a twelve-month period. The aim is to ensure that people from previously excluded ethnic minority groups can compete on equal terms with other applicants, making up for the accumulated effects of past discrimination.

However, the Race Relations Act does not allow positive discrimination or affirmative action. Selection itself must be based on merit and treat all applicants equally, so an employer cannot try to change the balance of the workforce by selecting someone mainly because she or he is from a particular racial group.

This begs the question – is anti-discrimination law flexible enough to secure equality, or do we need to start considering a role for exercising a preference for diversity in order to rebalance our workforces?

A number of public organisations – universities, police authorities and local authorities, for example – who regard greater diversity as essential to their operational success have drawn attention to the limits placed on them by equality legislation. Police forces are set recruitment targets by the Home Office (targets that, incidentally, most chief constables accept are necessary to achieve for *operational* reasons) but complain that the requirements of the Race Relations Act and the Sex Discrimination Act prevent them from taking actions that would help them to achieve these targets. Similarly, universities concerned that some of their courses are becoming predominantly female, to the exclusion of young White males, are concerned that they may not have the flexibility to make special provisions to encourage a more balanced intake.

Taking a look at the evidence bears out these concerns. Measuring the momentum with which some of the inequalities in Britain are being corrected presents a depressing picture.[78] For example, *at the current rate of change* we will only elect a representative House of Commons in 2080, close the gender pay gap in 2085, and close the ethnic employment gap in 2105. Ending the 50+ employment penalty is not likely to happen in this lifetime. We will probably never close the disability employment gap. And we will definitely never close the ethnic qualification gap – given the current rate of change in the wrong direction.

79 *Sex Discrimination (Election Candidates) Act 2002* (TSO, 2002).

Given the significance of the more intractable inequalities outlined above, the case for balancing measures to redress gaps between groups should be irresistible. However, the case is challenged by the difficulty of explaining the difference between measures intended to change outcomes for groups at an aggregate level, and the preferential treatment of individual members of particular groups. Preventing discrimination against individuals is, of course, important – but it will not shift mountains. The goal is to remedy disadvantage at a structural level by changing the framework in which decisions are made: for example, by examining how job entry systems affect different groups and taking steps to ensure that application and success rates are balanced. Tackling aggregate disadvantage requires us to recognise that disadvantage in the first place – to acknowledge that group poverty and inequality strip people of their individual capability to access the opportunities that are theoretically available to all. This is why treating people fairly does not always mean treating everyone the same.

What might balancing measures look like? Clearly they would have to vary to fit the circumstances of any particular problem. However, we have already seen measures taken to address the apparently intractable and clearly unjustifiable under-representation of women elected members in the House of Commons. In 2002, Parliament concluded that it had to give political parties more leeway to take special measures to change the gender balance of the candidates they put before the electorate.[79] Until 2015, the selection of election candidates by political parties has been exempted from certain aspects of the Sex Discrimination Act to enable positive action to try to ensure greater gender balance in political representation.

The important features of this exceptional step are that:

- it was introduced to remedy a clearly quantifiable equality gap that seemed impervious to other remedies;
- the inequality involved was widely held to have reduced the credibility and the effectiveness of the institution involved (including the House of Commons);

80 Op.cit., ref. 74.

- the relaxation of the law is not permanent; it was envisaged that when a more acceptable balance was achieved this special measure would lapse.

And it has made a significant difference, resulting in a far more representative House of Commons (albeit from a low base), which has greater legitimacy as a result.

But are we ready to take such drastic action on equality in other fields? At the moment, there is evidence to suggest that the British people are not yet prepared for the changes around the corner, or what they perforce mean for our attitudes towards inequality. There is little public agreement on what is meant by equality in practice. There is public commitment to the idea of fairness, but it is weakly supported or not well understood, in particular in relation to the allocation of public resource and political attention to equality measures. The *British Social Attitudes Survey* in 2004, for example, explored public attitudes to inequality of income in Britain. The survey showed that nearly three-quarters of respondents said that the gap between those with high and low incomes is too large; however only one-third of respondents agreed that government should redistribute incomes from one group to another.[80] Further exploration of the issues, however, showed that the picture is much more complex. Nearly nine in ten favoured tax and spending policies whose overall impact is clearly redistributive, including most of those who, when asked directly, did not explicitly support redistribution.

It appears that there is strong support for increased social justice and help for the more disadvantaged in society, but that this general feeling is not well articulated or translated into support for practical programmes. Worse still, in the absence of an agreed framework for discussion about equality, debates about priorities and policy can easily degenerate into unseemly competitions between groups of disadvantaged people, or into accusations of special pleading. A key problem for the Equalities Review, which I chair, is how to develop a modern case for equality, along with the language and concepts that we need in order to explain what the problem is, identify what needs to be done, and persuade the public of its importance (and its relevance to each person's life).

At the very least, I hope that the Equalities Review work will break open a debate on the meaning of equality in the 21st century so that we can start to see more clearly what all of it really means and how society needs to change. If not, the risk is that we will continue helplessly to produce ever-more umbrellas while the floodwaters creep up past our shoulders.

7. Aspiration and community[81]

Sir Jonathan Sacks

81 This chapter is extracted from J Sacks, 'Compassion: The idea of tzedakah' in *The Dignity of Difference: How to avoid the clash of civilizations,* (Continuum International Publishing Group Ltd, 2003): ISBN-10, 0826468500; ISBN-13, 978-0826468505; RRP: £7.99.

82 *Financial Times,* 6 November 2001.

The great concern of Moses was . . . to lay the foundation of a social state in which deep poverty and degrading want should be unknown.
Henry George, *Moses.*

'Think of a stretch limousine driving through an urban ghetto,' writes Martin Wolf of the *Financial Times.*[82] 'Inside is the post-industrial world of western Europe, North America, Australasia, Japan and the emerging Pacific Rim. Outside are all the rest.' That is what a globalised planet is rapidly becoming: one in which wealth is ever-more unevenly distributed, in which the rich get richer and the poor get poorer. Each year there are more billionaires. Each year millions die of starvation, poverty and preventable disease. That is the difference between micro- and macroeconomics. In each individual transaction, both sides gain. But when the results of billions of transactions are aggregated, their effects can be, and often are, massively inequitable. That is something globalisation has magnified, not diminished. It turns the planet into a single market with highly mobile funds and near-perfect information and competition. Investment moves from country to country, seeking maximal returns without regard to human consequences. Our world is getting less equal by the year.

That inequality exists both within and between countries. In the second half of the twentieth century, worldwide consumption of goods and services grew six-fold. But according to a United Nations survey, one-sixth of the world's population – a billion people – live on less than a dollar a day and cannot satisfy the most basic human needs. More than eight million die each year because of polluted water or contaminated air. Six million die from malnutrition or starvation. Two million die from diarrhoea or related diseases.[83] AIDS has already claimed the lives of ten million Africans and is projected to kill 25 million more in the next decade. Among the 4.5 billion inhabitants of developing countries, three in five lack access to basic infrastructure. A third have no drinkable water. A quarter live in substandard accommodation. A fifth have no sanitary or medical services. In Africa, the poorest region of the world, 174 of every thousand children fail to reach the age of five. A fifth of the world's children spend less than five years in school. The same percentage are permanently undernourished.[84]

And the gap grows. Between 1965 and 1999, real incomes per head in the developed countries rose by 2.4%. Those in the Middle East and North Africa stayed roughly the same. In sub-Saharan Africa they fell. Eighty-nine countries are worse off now than they were ten years ago. Thirty-five have experienced a greater fall than during the Great Depression of the 1930s. Worldwide, the top 20% of high-income earners account for 86% of all private consumption, while the poorest 20% account for only 1.3%. The richest fifth consume sixteen times more meat, seventeen times more energy and 145 times more cars than the poorest fifth. Sixty-five per cent of the world's population have never made a telephone call. Forty per cent have no access to electricity. Americans spend more on cosmetics, and Europeans on ice cream, than it would cost to provide schooling and sanitation for the two billion people who currently go without both.

It is morally impossible not to be troubled by the ever-growing gap between the few at the top and the many at the bottom of the economic ladder. What makes the present situation worse than in the past is that these inequalities are visible. When the horizons of the majority of mankind were limited to the next village or town, inequalities might exist throughout the world but few were aware of them on a daily basis. There were fabled lands where gold ran free, but that was somewhere else in a world of legends and dreams. The global media have transformed all this. Television has brought the world of the rich and famous to the most remote villages, while bringing images of hunger, famine, war and disease into our living rooms. We can

83 J Micklethwaite and A Woolridge, *A Future Perfect* (Random House, 2001) p. 256.

84 Z Bauman, 'Whatever Happened to Compassion' in T Bentley and D Stedman-Jones, *The Moral Universe* (Demos, 2001), pp. 51-6.

85 Op.cit., ref. 83.

86 J Stiglitz, 'Globalism's discontents' (*The American Prospect*, 13(1), 2002).

no longer claim that we did not know.

Nor are traditional defences of inequality sustainable today. The worldview of antiquity and the middle ages was built on the belief that differences in power, wealth and status were part of the ordained order. Status was a given of birth. Hierarchy was written into the fabric of the universe.

Why then does it continue? Many defenders of the new, globalised economy argue – rightly, in my view – that it is the best chance nations have of defeating poverty. Countries that have embraced it, most notably in South-East Asia, but also in South America, have prospered. So has India, which has developed a highly effective information-technology base. The economic reforms introduced by Deng Xiaoping in China in 1978 helped eight hundred million peasants to double their incomes in a mere six years. Seventy-six million Chinese moved out of poverty in the past decade alone.[85]

But not every nation has access to the new technologies. They are on the other side of the so-called digital divide. Nor have world economic policies always been to the benefit of the poorest. Nobel prize-winning economist Joseph Stiglitz, former chief economist of the World Bank, has been highly critical of international financial institutions for the way they have imposed inappropriate strategies on failing economies. Economic liberalisation can make the strong stronger but the weak weaker. Stiglitz compares some of the economic policies imposed by the International Monetary Fund on poor countries to setting small boats loose on a rough sea. Even if the boats are sound and well captained, they are likely to be hit broadside by a big wave and capsize.[86]

A world in which the few prosper and many starve offends against our deepest sense of fairness and human solidarity. You do not have to be a convinced egalitarian to know that disparities of this magnitude – vast, concentrated wealth alongside widespread suffering – is intolerable. The real problem, though, is one of responsibility. No one planned this outcome. It happened as a result of billions of transactions, investments and purchasing decisions. As Robert Reich reminds us:

The emergence of the global, high-tech economy seems largely out of anyone's hands. One development seems to have sparked the next, with-

out any clear decision having been made about consequences. No one explicitly decided that technologies of communication, transportation, and information would advance as quickly as they have. Or that these technologies would push the economy from large-scale production toward a wide array of innovative products and services, with easy switching to better ones… Nor, especially, did anyone decide to accept the downsides of all this progress. [87]

87 R Reich, *The Future of Success* (William Heinemann, 2001), p.230.

The invisible hand – the unanticipated outcome of a myriad actions and reactions – is not always benign.

There are no easy solutions, but there are hard questions. What is our responsibility to humanity as a whole? What bonds of obligation link us to those with whom we do not share a country, a political structure, a language or culture? What proportion of our wealth, if any, are we duty bound to share? The language of rights is not always helpful here, because rights presuppose a network of law and obligation that can implement them. A right is like a cheque: it has value only if there is a bank and an account against which it can be drawn. Without that it is mere expectation without delivery. What then is the moral basis of global economic responsibility?

At this level, religious concepts are more helpful than narrowly political or economic ones. The central insight of monotheism - that if God is the parent of humanity, then we are all members of a single extended family – has become more real in its implications than ever before. The Enlightenment gave us the concept of universal rights, but this remains a 'thin' morality, stronger in abstract ideas than in its grip on the moral imagination. Far more powerful is the biblical idea that those in need are our brothers and sisters and that poverty is something we feel in our bones. The great faiths do more than give abstract expression to our shared humanity; they move us to action and give compelling shape to the claims of others upon us.

I want to examine the Jewish experience because it combines two elements that are particularly relevant to our present situation. On the one hand, Judaism is sympathetic to the free market and limited government as the best defences of individual liberty and creativity. On the other, it was aware from the days of Moses that an open economy does not guarantee just outcomes in the larger sense of a society in which everyone has the

88 N Gottwald, *The Tribes of Yahweh* (SCM Press, 1980), p. 699.

89 Ibid, p. 700.

means of a dignified existence. This, to Moses and the prophets, was a matter of deep concern. In the words of one contemporary biblical scholar: 'From the start, Israel lived with a covenant charter which put optimum value on a people in egalitarian relations under one sovereign divine power.'[88] Early Israelite religion was the attempt to create a 'heterogeneous, classless, decentralized association of tribes conceived as a brotherhood – and at least in larger measure than in Canaanite society, as a sisterhood – of social, economic and political equals.'[89] That involved a commitment, one we can trace through biblical legislation and prophetic utterance to an economic order that balanced freedom with equity. To understand it, we must first understand the idea contained in one of Judaism's key words.

In two verses in the book of Genesis, God specifies the mission with which Abraham and his descendants are to be charged:

Shall I hide from Abraham what I am about to do? Abraham will surely become a great and powerful nation, and all nations of the earth will be blessed through him. For I have chosen him so that he will direct his children and his household after him to keep the way of the Lord by doing what is right [tzedakah] *and just* [mishpat]*, so that the Lord will bring about for Abraham what He has promised him.* (Genesis *18:17-19*)

The two words, *tzedakah* and *mishpat,* signify different forms of justice. *Mishpat* means retributive justice or the rule of law. A free society must be governed by law, impartially administered, through which the guilty are punished, the innocent acquitted, and human rights secured. *Tzedakah,* by contrast, refers to distributive justice, a less procedural and more substantive idea.

It is difficult to translate *tzedakah* because it combines in a single word two notions normally opposed to one another, namely charity and justice. Suppose, for example, that I give someone £100. Either he is entitled to it, or he is not. If he is, then my act is a form of justice. If he is not, it is an act of charity. In English (as with the Latin terms *caritas* and *iustitia*) a gesture of charity cannot be an act of justice, nor can an act of justice be described as charity. *Tzedakah* is therefore an unusual term, because it means both.

It arises from the theology of Judaism, which insists on the difference between possession and ownership. Ultimately, all things are owned by God, creator of the world. What we possess, we do not own – we merely hold it in trust for God. The clearest example is the provision in Leviticus: 'The land must not be sold permanently because the land is Mine; you are merely strangers and temporary residents in relation to Me' (*Leviticus* 25:23). If there were absolute ownership, there would be a difference between justice (what we are bound to give others) and charity (what we give others out of generosity). The former would be a legally enforceable duty, the latter, at most, a moral obligation, the prompting of benevolence or sympathy. In Judaism, however, because we are not owners of our property but merely guardians on God's behalf, we are bound by the conditions of trusteeship, one of which is that we share part of what we have with others in need. What would be regarded as charity in other legal systems is, in Judaism, a strict requirement of the law and can, if necessary, be enforced by the courts.

What *tzedakah* signifies, therefore, is what is often called 'social justice', meaning that no one should be without the basic requirements of existence, and that those who have more than they need must share some of that surplus with those who have less. This is absolutely fundamental to the kind of society the Israelites were charged with creating, namely one in which everyone has a basic right to a dignified life and to be equal citizens in the covenantal community under the sovereignty of God. So, for example, the covenant code specifies:

> *Do not ill-treat a stranger [i.e. a non-Israelite] or oppress him, for you were strangers in the land of Egypt.*
> *Do not take advantage of a widow or orphan. If you do, and they cry out to Me, I will certainly hear their cry . . .*
> *If you lend money to one of My people among you who is needy, do not be like a money-lender: charge him no interest.*
> *If you take your neighbour's cloak as a pledge, return it to him by sunset, because his cloak is the only covering he has for his body. What else will he sleep in? When he cries out to Me, I will hear, for I am compassionate.* (Exodus 22:21-27)

God, for the Israelites, was actively concerned in the economic

90 A Sen, *Development as Freedom* (Oxford University Press, 1999), p. 284.

and political order, especially with those who, because they lacked power, or even a 'voice', became the victims of injustice and inequity:

He upholds the cause of the oppressed,
And gives food to the hungry.
The Lord sets prisoners free.
The Lord gives sight to the blind,
The Lord lifts up those who are bowed down,
The Lord loves the righteous.
The Lord watches over the stranger,
And sustains the fatherless and the widow,
But He frustrates the way of the wicked. (Psalm *146: 7-9*)

The society the Israelites were to construct would stand as a living contrast to what they experienced in Egypt: poverty, persecution and enslavement. Their release from bondage was only the first stage on their journey to freedom. The second – their covenant with God – involved collective responsibility to ensure that no one would be excluded from the shared graciousness of the community and its life. Hence the Bible's insistence that a free society cannot be built on *mishpat,* the rule of law, alone. It requires also *tzedakah,* a just distribution of resources. This view has close affinities with Nobel Prize-winning economist Amartya Sen's concept of 'development as freedom':

The adult who lacks the means of having medical treatment for an ailment from which she suffers is not only prey to preventable morbidity and possibly escapable mortality, but may also be denied the freedom to do various things – for herself and for others – that she may wish to do as a responsible human being. The bonded labourer born into semi-slavery, the subjugated girl child stifled by a repressive society, the helpless landless labourer without substantial means of earning an income are all deprived not only in terms of well-being, but also in terms of the ability to lead responsible lives, which are contingent on having certain basic freedoms. Responsibility *requires* freedom.[90]

Sen has, I believe, put it absolutely correctly. *Individual* freedom may be best described, as Isaiah Berlin argued, in terms of 'negative liberty', namely the absence of constraints (*chofesh* in biblical Hebrew). But *collective* freedom (*cherut* in Hebrew) is something else. It means, among other things, that my freedom is not bought at the price of yours. A society in which the few prosper but the many starve, in which some but not all have access to good education, health care, and other essential amenities, is not a place of liberty. That requires more than an absence of coercion. It involves the removal of barriers to the exercise of responsible citizenship: 'poverty as well as tyranny, poor economic opportunities as well as systematic social deprivation, neglect of public facilities as well as intolerance or overactivity of repressive states.'[91]

With the transition, some two thousand years ago, from biblical to post-biblical Judaism, we find a greater emphasis on *tzedakah,* the direct provision of financial aid, as opposed to agricultural produce. Israel had become less of an agrarian economy, more a society of small businesses and trade, and rabbinic law is a systematic attempt to apply the principles of the Bible to new economic circumstances. Communal taxes were instituted. New forms of distribution were set up, among them the *tamchui,* which distributed food daily, and the *kuppah,* which weekly provided funds for those in need. The disbursement of *tzedakah* funds called for high standards of probity, so to be appointed as a distributor of communal funds became one of the highest accolades the community could give.

The key text here was Deuteronomy 15:8: 'You shall open your hand wide to him [the poor person] and shall surely lend him sufficient for his need in that which he lacks.' The rabbis took this to include gifts as well as loans. More importantly, they read it as offering a definition of the kinds of poverty they were called on to address:

Sufficient for his need – *means that you are commanded to maintain him, but you are not commanded to make him rich.* That which he lacks – *means even a horse to ride on and a slave to run before him. It is told of Hillel the elder [head of the Jewish community in the first century BCE] that he bought for a certain poor man of good family a horse to ride on and a slave to run before him. On one occasion he could not find a slave to run before him, so he himself ran before him for three miles.*[92]

There are two kinds of poverty according to this interpretation.

91 ibid., p. 3.

92 Babylonian Talmud, *Ketubot*, p. 67b.

The first ('sufficient for his need') refers to an absolute subsistence level. In Jewish law this was taken to include food, housing, basic furniture and, if necessary, funds to pay for a wedding. The second ('that which he lacks') means relative poverty – relative, however, not to others but to the individual's own previous standard of living. This is the first indication of something that plays an important role in the rabbinic understanding of poverty. Over and above sheer physical needs is a psychological dimension. Poverty *humiliates,* and a good society will not allow humiliation.

Judaism represents a highly distinctive approach to the idea of equality, namely that it is best served not by equality of income or wealth, nor even of opportunity. Nor is it sufficient that we each have equal standing before God at times of prayer, and before the law in cases of dispute. A society must ensure equal dignity – the Hebrew phrase is *kavod habriyot,* 'human honour' – to each of its members.

The prophets, who lived and worked more than two-and-a-half thousand years ago, were the world's first social critics, unashamed to deliver their message to kings and speak truth to power. Religion has, they argued, a moral, social and economic dimension. It involves justice, not merely in the narrow sense of the rule of law and the transparency of procedures, but also in the substantive sense of conferring on all members of society an honoured place. And what, in the days of the prophets, applied socially, today applies globally. The scope of our interconnectedness defines the radius of responsibility and concern.

Tzedakah is a concept for our time. The retreat from a welfare state set in motion by Reagonomics and Thatcherism, together with the deregulation of financial markets throughout the world, have led to increased and increasing inequalities in both developed countries and the developing world. The importance of tzedakah is that it does not mean 'charity'. It is not optional, nor does it depend on the goodwill of those who give to others. It is a legally enforceable obligation. Nor does it depend on any specific economic doctrine. It goes hand in hand with a free market, while recognising that the market has inherent limits. George Soros is right when he admits that: 'International trade and global financial markets are very good at generating wealth, but they cannot take care of other social needs, such as the preservation of peace, alleviation of poverty, protection of the environment, labor conditions, or human rights – what are generally called "public goods".[93]

The inequities of markets are no reason to abandon the market. Globalisation has led to increased prosperity for those countries who have participated in it. We will not cure poverty by destroying a system of wealth-creation, any more than we will cure illness by abolishing doctors or end crime by annulling law. New technologies and the growth of trade are our best – our only – hope for ending hunger, curing disease and raising living standards throughout the world. This, the rabbis recognised. The Talmud imagines the following dialogue between King David and his advisers:

At dawn, the wise men of Israel came to David and said, 'O Lord, the king, your people Israel need sustenance.' He said, 'Let them support one another.' They replied, 'A handful cannot satisfy a lion, and you cannot fill a pit by the earth which you dig from it.'[94]

David proposed redistribution. His sages told him that the cake was not big enough, however it was sliced. Economic growth is more powerful than simple redistribution. But that is true only if there is a genuine willingness on the part of those who gain to ensure that the losers also benefit; and that does not happen through the market mechanism on its own.

No religion can propose precise policies for the alleviation of hunger and disease. What it can do, and must, is to inspire us collectively with a vision of human solidarity and with concepts, such as *tzedakah* within the Jewish tradition and its counterparts in other faiths, that serve as a broad moral template for what constitutes a fair and decent world. Globalisation, writes Zygmunt Bauman, 'divides as much as it unites… signalling a new freedom for some, upon many others it descends as an uninvited and cruel fate.'[95] There can be no doubt that more – much more – of the economic surplus of advanced economies should be invested in developing countries to help eradicate extremes of poverty and hunger, ensure universal education, combat treatable disease, reduce infant mortality, improve work conditions and reconstruct failing economies. As with tzedakah, the aim should be to restore dignity and independence to

93 G Soros, *The Crisis of Global Capitalism* (Little, Brown & Co, 2002), p. 14

94 Babylonian Talmud, *Berakhoto* 3b.

95 Z Bauman, *Globalisation: The human consequences* (Polity Press, 1998), p. 2.

nations as well as individuals. This has now become an urgent imperative. The globalisation of communications, trade and culture, globalises human responsibility likewise. The freedom of the few may not be purchased at the price of the enslavement of the many to poverty, ignorance and disease.

Two case studies: making a difference

8: The gateless wall: a discourse on participation

Camila Batmanghelidjh

We live in an age where there is intense preoccupation about legitimate participation. Those with power to make decisions and create social policies have promised themselves that they will include the excluded. Agencies have been created to achieve the inclusion agenda. The social exclusion and social inclusion ministries lead, with their varied metamorphoses, following in hot pursuit. In education, culture, sports, regeneration and media, inclusion is the Holy Grail.

However, despite such aspiration, there remains something of a *diss-ease*. From the streets where Kids Company operates, supporting 11,000 vulnerable children and families, the inclusion agenda appears to be failing. One in five children suffer from emotional and mental health difficulties. The bulk of the academies, with their computers and buildings boasting 'state-of-the-art', are still struggling to achieve academically. There is also a significant youth crime problem: children are killing, stealing, and creating ghettos in which they victimise themselves and visitors who cross the path. The hostels and the housing estates boast drug economies, which surpass in profit some of the FTSE top 100 companies.

The inclusion agenda may be failing for a number of reasons, some of which I'd like to explore in this paper.

I have chosen the title of 'The gateless wall', but it could either be bricked up with no entry, or have a path through that is so clearly unavailable for the passing that a gate is not needed. I believe that the inclusion agenda is being conceived in such a flawed way that, unwittingly, it has generated a brick wall, creating divisions.

Divisions emerge when situations are split into those who act and those who are subjects, or subjected, to that action. Intrinsic in this kind of structure is a power imbalance, with one half being recipients of the other half's 'gifts'. What gets missed is mutual participation. This divide is unwittingly generated because those who have comfortable and choice-plenty opportunities first feed their own needs, and then gather what they have spare in order to share it with those who have not. The decision, the distribution of favours and goods, is primarily with the giver, and the recipient has to make good use passively and be appreciative of what has been given to them.

The brick wall separating the two emanates from a compassion-negative position. In genuine compassion there is a fusion between care-giver and care-recipient whereby, at the point of alleviating suffering or creating potentials together, they are uniformly equalised and united in the moment. The moment is when mind, action, spirit and event are mutually perceived and shared. For compassion to be at its most effective, the individualist ego of both care-giver and recipient is overridden by an understanding of a shared task and goal.

The current social inclusion agenda, I would argue, is failing because it is compassion-negative. It is morally and philosophically flawed, and it lacks humility on the part of the care-giver. The arrogance presents itself because the care-giver is setting the care-recipient an agenda of achievement that is relevant to the 'I' worldview rather than to the 'your' or 'our joint' worldview. The 'I' worldview believes that the space the care-giver is residing in has superior qualities, which the care-recipient must be elevated to. To those ends, the care-giver identifies for the care-recipient the targets that have to be met. This is manifest in every aspect of the social inclusion agenda. In education, it is about levels of literacy, numeracy and the rat race of league tables. In culture, it's the tick-box tyranny of getting ethnic minorities, people with disabilities, and every slice of exclusion manifestation through the gallery and museum doors. In business, it's about forcing employees to make one day's contact with that 'other world', so that the organisation can boast its corporate social responsibility manifestation in its annual report – to the condescending nod of the shareholders.

Nothing is sadder than the perversion of inclusion that has become an industry, as it is sarcastically viewed from the ghettos. As this florid action and expenditure cajoles to elevate the ghetto to perceived levels of excellence, the brick wall separating the two thickens and mutual rage seeps through across the divide.

What would make the space gateless, and allow genuine access? In the spirit of making theory manifest in practice, I'm going to help you enter the worldview of the children Kids Company works with. I often hear providers protest that so much opportunity is made available to these young people, yet these providers do not engage and participate. If a provider entered one of these children's world-spaces the comprehension would make visible the barriers to participation.

We at Kids Company began to understand the process of alienation only when we agreed to be 'in community' with these young people; it meant spending time with them, listening to them, travelling to the places they went, and sharing with them their emotional experiences. What we learned is that the ability to participate requires an emotional readiness and availability, all of us do not come to the point of opportunity with the same prerequisites.

Children who have grown up in conditions of terror develop hyper-vigilance and a chemistry of urgency. As toddlers they are helpless and passive bystanders who witness domestic violence, crazed and dangerous behaviour – the terrorised imprinting of horrific images dominates their brain and emotional space. Initially the bystander child is damaged and the powerlessness leaves a legacy of humiliation. The profound sense of having no impact on preventing violence towards others, and towards the self, brings the vulnerable child defencelessly into contact with a sense of catastrophic redundancy. The only ammunition against such overpowering experiences while you are small is to switch off the ability to feel. In being numb, the child ceases to protest and occupies a dead space where there is neither a striving for life, nor a seeking of death. The neutralised child separates from the human world and becomes a far-away emotional island.

Sometimes, as these children grow up, their physical bellies rumble for food and they reach a primitive perception of the world as a space in which you have to survive through your own initiative because no one takes responsibility for protecting you or honouring your childhood. The child, savaged, will learn the currency of cruelty in order to make a shift from victim to perpetrator – from underdog to top dog. Place a young person whose mindset is about survival in an academy where the agenda is aspiration, and you place him in front of a gateless brick wall, because there's a disjuncture between his worldview and your worldview.

This child is astute enough to comprehend that the legitimate world you represent and embody is the space of power, honour and achievement. The child looks on and realises that in comparison, and in your eyes, because he or she cannot operate through your worldview he is smaller than you and powerless in relation to your structure. The power discrepancy accelerates the experience of humiliation and the child, yet again, is plunged into a fight-flight expression. The flight is the self-exclusion, the truancy and the avoidance. The fight is redefining the currency of power by creating an agenda within the school culture where his brand of power, achieved through violence, becomes a perverse and illegitimate structure within which he is superior. A dichotomy of potency is created within the school. The aspirational worldview proposes power through achievement, sticking to rules and participation. The illegitimate power structure demands destruction, breaking rules and being empowered through violence.

Who is going to be the winner? Invariably the one who has managed to give up the most is the one who becomes the most powerful. The suicidally powerful child, in giving up the will to self-preserve, acquires a potency that comes of being able to negate the self, not because it's a sacrifice, but because trauma has made the self so meaningless as to not be worth preserving.

The achiever, on the other hand, has been fed with a worldview in which he has become the commodity; attainment and status are sought in order for the human being to become a desirable object. Sadly, this too is survival behaviour. Lack of achievement risks making the individual not worthy of being chosen. Both the achiever and the non-achiever in this scenario reside in a space where there is a negation of being for being's sake - that is, for the sake of connecting, for the sake of loving, for sharing humanity, for participating in mutually creative tasks. Both sets of children experience a brick wall. One is defined as the social failure, the other is paraded as social success, but both represent a profound perversion of human and humanitarian values.

This abusive cycle is further perpetuated by those who fund social intervention initiatives, and often those who deliver them. The business representative travels to the ghettos heavy with his egocentric philanthropy. He too brings his worldview to the situation. He seeks a legacy, a personal definition of quality, which his money must buy. In his helping glance the recipient is turned into an object upon which he's going to act his sense of power and potency. He wants outcomes, tangible, manifest on the page; sometimes he wants objects like computers or a building that never escape the memory of his donation. And like a grovelling beggar, humiliated and trapped into this vision, the social catalysts distort the spirit of their work. Similarly, they turn the client into an object for the collusive outcome desired, because the money is needed and the donor has to be pleased. Truth and courage are compromised, and a rift is generated as the recipient's needs no longer form the centre of the creative task, but the donor's need takes precedent.

You may well interject, why can't both their needs be met simultaneously? They can, but that's a transaction. It's not compassion or the expression of it. The mutuality does not evolve around the most urgent need; it evolves around an exchange of commodities.

A concrete understanding of opportunities also manifests itself in the equality agenda. The best understanding of equality, paradoxically, rests in embracing diversity. The individual is perceived as unique, needing equally individually tailored interventions and opportunities. The equality agenda becomes destructive when it is represented as equal opportunities, i.e. the

96 A Maslow, *Motivation and Personality,* (Harper & Row, 2nd ed. 1970).

same for everyone. In homogenisation there is an equally anti-compassion agenda whereby the opportunity becomes dominant into which the individual must be accommodated. This type of thinking creates a brick wall while attempting to remove barriers to access.

As the child's most urgent requirements are not addressed, the child is left humiliated and further alienated. Opportunities look toxic; they are meaningless offerings because they miss his meaning of the moment. On both sides of the wall anger resides. The opportunity-providers experience frustration as their aspirational offerings are not taken up. The recipient is described as unappreciative, lacking in aspiration, and intrinsically seeking failure. It is never acknowledged that in not providing appropriate and meaningful interventions the failure resides with the opportunity-providers. Simultaneously, the failed and vulnerable child takes on board the mismatch between personal need and the provision of resources as a statement of personal flaw. Self-esteem is further diminished, humiliation strengthened and the despair grips, suffocatingly, pulling the child further into exclusion.

Whose responsibility is it to repair this dynamic? Who should take the initiative to exercise compassion? Who should step away from their worldview into the other? Opportunity-providers often argue that the excluded should be more proactive: 'get on your bike and get a job'. Abraham Maslow, in the 1960s, contributed to the answer. He conceived of a triangle, the pinnacle of which was self-actualisation – the space of aspirational thinking. But he made it clear that unless the needs lower down the triangle were met, self-actualisation was not possible. The bottom of the triangle began with a need for food and safety, then a need for love further up and, when those primary physical and psychological thirsts had been quenched, the personal 'I' could look beyond itself to self-actualisation – a space where fulfilment allows the negation or rising above the self into a space of mutuality; where the personal, the divine and the other are not separated. [96]

The compassionate person exercises the ability to self-actualise but in the reverse. Rather than going up the triangle, the self-actualised agree to travel down it, in order to meet a fellow human being at a point of need. The gift is in being able to leave the self or rise beyond it and share, or be in a common space with another. The exhilaration is in the empathic experience. The living absolutely, undividedly, the moment where the opportunity-provider and the recipient are not separated. The mutuality of the experience has no room for power discrepancies, and therefore there is no humiliation; no one is trapped, powerless, in the eyes of the powerful. Both are equally engaged around a task – the act of help from the perspective of the recipients' worldview.

If the education provider could show curiosity as to why the pupil cannot make use of the opportunity, if there could be a suspension of judgment, if the intelligence in every piece of action could be respected, then the 'urgent child' would be able to explain that he does not come to the classroom with a psychological and emotional chemistry ready to take in the learning. Perhaps he would like to explain that he hates being a recipient, taking learning in, feels like an intrusion reminding him of the unwanted penetration of his childhood sexual abuse or the force-feeding of his crazed mother. He needs somewhere safe where the barrel of the drug dealer's gun is not chasing him. Perhaps he feels too fragile, tentatively glued together in an encapsulated space to which he is frightened of allowing entry, for fear of being fragmented. Maybe being present in the classroom feels like being on display – all eyes noticing, registering, the flawed presence, the persecutory voices of outsiders have now internalised into a tirade of self-hate, and every teacher's glance is embroiled into the drama of shame. Perhaps he might want to let them know that he cannot be in the classroom for fear that his mother's boyfriend may harm her, or his drug-addicted father may suffocate in his own unprocessed vomit.

These are the preoccupations of the violated child whose classroom engagement is interfered with. But equally painful and poignant are the psychological disruptions experienced by children whose practical life circumstances may not be as visibly terrorising. The fear they harbour might be about not living up to expectations, being terrified of being unloved because they are not becoming the objects of aspirational fantasy – their parents' project. All these children have so much to share with us about the barriers to accessing opportunities, if only we had room to listen.

The richness and the aspiration that the opportunity-provider is seeking, the absolute sense of excellence and quality are mistakenly being pursued in the league tables. And yet perhaps it resides somewhere only humility can genuinely access, and in finding it one may be propelled into levels of excellence that are beyond the control-freakery masquerading as achievement.

So what makes the wall gateless and the path a meeting point? More than the computer and the state-of-the-art building, these children seek compassion. They need loving care from the soothing of which they can learn to calm themselves down. They need to be embraced from the ostracisation. Compassion, in the expression of which profound love is experienced; in the moment, when there is mutual experience of love there cannot be exclusion as there is no duality, no divide.

9. The experience of Ninestiles School: a case study in making an educational difference

Sir Dexter Hutt

Educational disadvantage need not be self-perpetuating: there are many individual examples of working class parents and first generation immigrant parents with limited education themselves whose children have been successful in our education system. But in the past this has been largely due to the determination and aspiration of these parents and often in spite of, rather than because of, our education system.

There has always been a moral imperative for fairness in life chances of all children, but this has not been enough to generate determination and aspiration on a national scale. Grammar schools provided a lifeline for some, but implicit in that system was an acceptance that the majority could be left with a level of education that would enable them to survive but not to progress much beyond their parents' achievements. Until 1972 many could, and did, leave school at the age of fifteen. Unskilled jobs were relatively plentiful and many (particularly boys) could and did follow their fathers into the traditional industries, like mining, shipbuilding and the car industry.

It was James Callaghan's Ruskin College speech in October 1976 that signalled the beginnings of a step change in national determination and aspiration, and much has happened since then with much increased government investment in schools, accompanied by unprecedented accountability through public inspections and public league tables. And, overall, standards have risen significantly, with currently 62% of our population achieving five or more good GCSE passes at age sixteen. But that still leaves 38% of our students with a level of education that is unlikely to do much for their life chances. And the majority of these are to be found among the most disadvantaged sections of society.

Luckily for the current generation, the 21st century challenges are focusing our thinking. Sir Digby Jones, speaking at the end of 2005 in his role as Director General of the CBI, argued that the nineteenth century belonged to Britain, the twentieth century belonged to the United States, and the 21st century will belong to Asia. He went on to make the point that we can either equip ourselves, or we can leave our economy to a cold and frightening future. Equipping ourselves must surely include building an education system that reaches further and deeper than ever before – an education system that results in the *average* education level of our population being significantly higher to support the development of skills appropriate to Britain's needs in the 21st century.

So the good news is that the economic imperative has arrived and for the first time in our history has combined with the ever-present moral imperative to raise our determination and aspiration for *all* of the current and future generations. Witness the government's Every Child Matters agenda. But can we meet the challenge of raising the education level of our remaining 38% – among them the most disadvantaged sections of our society? How might we need to restructure our school system to make Every Child Matters a reality? And what lessons might we learn from pockets of existing school practice where disadvantage has been overcome?

In 1988, a third of the students leaving Ninestiles School in the Acocks Green area of Birmingham left without a single GCSE pass; 9% of students left with five or more A - C passes. But in 2006, 82% of students gained five or more A* - C passes and Ninestiles was one of only two secondary schools in the region (the other one was a boys' grammar school) identified by Ofsted as having had two consecutive outstanding inspections. Since 2001, Ninestiles has been accountable for three other secondary schools, all serving disadvantaged communities. Each of the three schools in turn became the most improved in their local authority. So what have been the key strategic ingredients behind the improvement of these schools? And can they be replicated on a wider scale?

Ninestiles in 1988 existed in a different educational world, with little public accountability and very limited support from the local authority or the government. It was probably typical of many schools serving disadvantaged communities. The physical environment was poor – a run-down 1928 building, walls with peeling paint, rotting window frames and flat roofs that leaked in many places. Teachers were happy with no sense of failure because of the overriding belief – common at that time – that schools could not overcome disadvantage and were victims of the areas that they served. Low expectations and little challenge from the local authority reinforced this belief. Ninestiles was heavily undersubscribed, with the majority of aspiring parents in the area understandably choosing to send their sons and daughters elsewhere. The school tried to do its best by working to a rigidly streamed system, separating pupils by perceived ability into separate teaching groups. This enabled students who were considered to have potential to be taught in a separate top stream, and the school's expectations of examination outcomes were inevitably focused on this group of 30 or so students. The result was a powerful self-labelling culture, with both students and teachers being labelled according to the stream they were in or that they taught. There was little incentive for teachers to work in teams or to reflect on teaching and learning. Outside of the top stream the vast majority of students responded to the low expectations with poor motivation and even poorer behaviour. Unsurprisingly, social relationships between students were poor: fighting, swearing and racist name calling were prevalent. Parental expectation outside of the top stream was also very low – it was not uncommon for students to leave at the Easter of their final year to take up unskilled jobs, often with the encouragement of their parents. The result in terms of examination outcomes was a self-fulfilling prophecy.

The new head who arrived in April 1988 identified improving social relationships as the key platform for improving motivation and raising expectation, and the streamed system as the major structural block to this happening. HMI (Her Majesty's Inspector of schools) was asked to recommend schools with good mixed ability practice in the different subject areas, and teams of teachers sent to visit these schools. In September 1988 the streamed structure was dismantled and replaced with a mixed ability system. At the same time, the pastoral support was restructured to enable heads of year to move up with their students and have the opportunity to build relationships with parents over the five years of secondary schooling.

The practice of teachers working largely on their own was changed by establishing faculty teams, with faculty heads made accountable not just for their own teaching but for that of all their team. Expectations of middle managers were made clear. Lesson observations were also introduced, with teachers learning from watching each other teach and beginning to support each other. It was made clear that this was going to be an open culture characterised by accountability rather than blame. Teachers needing support were encouraged to seek help from their colleagues, and more skilled teachers were asked to help others. And it was also made clear that those who were not interested in improving their teaching skills should look elsewhere for employment. Some teachers left willingly, others required strong encouragement. But the overwhelming majority stayed and became increasingly reflective about their own practice. Students responded positively to the better planned lessons. A spiral of rising expectations among both teachers and students began to emerge.

Parental expectations were tackled through face-to-face meetings with parents at school and through home visiting, and photographs of *every* student who achieved were displayed in prominent areas so that they could not be missed by parents who attended parents' evenings and other such occasions. Parental expectation began to change as parents recognised the faces of achieving students who lived in the same street or had come from the same primary school as their own child.

Senior staff appointed from within responded positively to the changes, and two new appointments at deputy head level were critical to maintaining the momentum. Senior team residential weekends to discuss and plan the school's annual priorities within a rolling three-year developmental plan built up team spirit, a shared vision and a 'can do' culture. Whole-school policies were agreed and then teams given the freedom to be creative *within the agreed framework.* Innovation began to flourish. And recruitment became easier as both experienced and younger teachers were attracted by the school's momentum and willingness to embrace change. Jim Collins, author of the best-selling management book *Good to Great,* would argue that we were getting the right people on the bus.[97]

97 J Collins, *Good to Great* (HarperCollins, 2001).

The task of school leadership is to create a climate that teachers will respond to. Step one is to establish a platform of order that can support teaching and learning. It is highly demotivating for teachers to spend hours planning lessons and then find that they are unable to deliver them because of poor behaviour in the classroom. Most schools have behaviour policies in theory but, in practice, the teacher in a classroom has to establish his or her own discipline. Ninestiles supported its teachers by implementing a whole-school discipline policy, behaviour for learning (BFL). Clear, simple rules for the classroom and movement around the school were introduced and explained to students. Breaking the rules resulted in sequential consequences of increasing severity – the first two consequences were simply warnings, but consequence three resulted in a one-hour detention. The key difference with other systems was that this detention was viewed as a sanction given by the teacher *on behalf of the school.* Detentions were therefore carried out centrally and supervised by a rota of teachers with all staff, including the head teacher, on the rota. Any student missing a detention was immediately followed up. It was important that BFL was perceived by students as consistent and fair – teachers were not allowed to 'jump' consequences, and students had the right of appeal. BFL was mirrored by a sequential praise system. Meetings were held with parents to explain the new behaviour system – this was a success and, indeed, some parents decided to adopt a similar approach at home.

The school's poor physical environment was improved. The building was painted, inside and outside, and leaking roofs repaired. Classrooms and corridors were carpeted. Toilets were refurbished. Display was given a high priority. This undoubtedly engendered a sense of pride among both staff and students, and added to the momentum of change. And it was a highly visible signal to parents and visitors that the school was changing. Changing the physical environment helped to raise expectations.

Staff made increasing use of data to track pupil progress and to give pupils regular feedback on their progress. Teachers moved away from the generality of 'work harder' to offering subject-specific advice to students on what they needed to do to move up to the next national curriculum level. And the concept of 'working at grades' was introduced to GCSE students. This was different from the usual forecast grade. Instead, seven times during the two years of the course we asked teachers to assess the work that students had done to date, treating the part of the syllabus covered as if it were the whole of the GCSE. Each student then received their current set of working at grades, and this was followed up with a personal interview and advice on how to improve their grades in each subject. Students found this highly motivating. Each set of working at grades was then analysed in terms of overall results in each subject and in terms of the whole school five or more A*-C and A*-G grades. The power of working at grades is that the analysis prompted intervention at every stage – at individual student level, faculty level and whole-school level. It enabled the school's leadership to highlight areas of concern and to focus on identified students, identified classes and identified subjects. Interventions included additional parental meetings, the introduction of after-school classes and classes during the holiday periods. And many teachers came in voluntarily to take Saturday morning classes. Students became excited by their progress between sets of working at grades. The final set of grades just before students sat their exams were virtually a forecast grade, since by that time the whole of the syllabus was covered. And the dominant emotion when results day dawned on the third Thursday in August was delight rather than surprise.

Underpinning all of our initiatives was the recognition that the school needed to win the hearts and minds of its students. The strategy for this was to take a service approach to students, role-playing the daily school experience from the students' point of view. Teachers talked with students and listened to them. The school day was radically reorganised and a staggered morning break and lunchtime introduced. This meant that the whole school were not trying to get served at the same time. We promised students a queuing time of not more than five minutes, and made this possible by increasing the number of serving points and tills. A cashless system also reduced the queuing time. Morning break was abandoned in favour of morning breakfast, with students choosing between cereals and a full English breakfast. Boys playing football tended to dominate the play areas, so the school quad became a girls'-only area. Lockers for all students meant they had somewhere to keep their personal possessions – it also meant that they did not have to carry their coats and heavy sets of books from classroom to classroom. A student phone was installed. Students had access to the library/ open learning centre before and after school. The equivalent of a customer services centre – a student support centre staffed by two support staff throughout the day, and the first port of call for any student with a problem or a need – was an immediate success. Daily whole-school assemblies with the whole student population in two sittings were introduced, enabling the school's values to be reinforced on every working day. Staff delivering high quality assemblies that students looked forward to became the norm.

Leaving arrangements for year eleven students are a very good indicator of any school's culture. At the start, like many schools, Ninestiles resorted to tricking students about the leaving day, fearful that they would take the opportunity to get their own back on a school that they did not like. Much progress has been made since those days! Now the leaving day is publicised well in advance, and students themselves organise their leaving assembly to take the form of a concert with performances by their peers. They then get very dressed up in eveningwear for their prom at a hotel. And the tears that flow freely, both at the leaving assembly and at the evening prom, are of joy and friendship rather than frustration.

Summarising the above, the key ingredients in effecting school improvement at Ninestiles were: a focus on building good social relationships within the school community; establishing an open, blame-free but highly accountable culture, which encourages risk taking and innovation; establishing teaching teams that are led as well as managed; a culture of high expectations and a shared vision that is understood by all;

strong leadership to get the right people in the right posts; making a statement with the physical environment; bringing parents on board with the school's initiatives; implementing an effective discipline system mirrored with a praise system; giving students subject-specific rather than just general advice; using data to monitor student progress and to identify where intervention is needed; using the service approach to win the hearts and minds of students.

Ninestiles has employed a combination of the above at three other schools serving highly disadvantaged communities that are or have been members of its federation over the last six years. It has been able to do so because it has been contractually accountable for the improvement of these schools. The combination that effectively gives the school its improvement strategy is a question of judgement and will vary depending on the phase that a particular school is in. The first federation school improved its five or more A*-C results from 16% to 75% over four years, the second school from 9% to 51% over three years. The third school, Central Technology College in Gloucester, a member of the federation from January 2006, improved its five or more A*-C pass rate from 24% to 49% in the six-month period to August 2006, making it the most improved school in the county.

We can conclude that schools serving disadvantaged communities can improve and the rate of improvement is likely to be more rapid if they are supported by a successful school with an understanding of school improvement strategies. This arrangement increases both the leadership and risk-taking capacity of the school. It also provides a pool of teaching expertise that can be used to support the disadvantaged school. But to be effective, the partnership does need to be a formal one with built-in accountability. Government policies that support such structured and accountable partnerships could make a significant contribution to ensuring that for many children educational disadvantage is not self-perpetuating.